NWADINOBI: The Tsetse Fly on the Scrotum

The Anathema of a Community

Korieocha Emmanuel Uwaozuruonye

Human Change Communications Company

H3cpublishers@yahoo.com

ISBN: 9789789980154

The wicked are estranged from the womb: they go astray as soon as they are born, speaking lies. Their poison is like the poison of a serpent: they are like the deaf adder that stops up her ear, which will not harken to the voice of charmers, charming never so wisely?
Psalm 58: 3-5

Confidence in fetishism is like chewing with a broken tooth or walking with a foot out of joint

Dedication

This work is dedicated to Almighty God for His mercy, grace and love.

My late mother, Appolonia Korieocha for igniting the candle of success for her children.

My late father, Elder Josiah Korieocha for his gold-dust inspiring parenthood.

Preface

This melodrama with fictitious characters depicts a paradoxical illusion in fiction.
The earth, the firmament and even the heavens shudder at the birth of every child. All ponders; looking morose at nothingness, for none can clairvoyantly ascertain the inherent trait (benevolent or malevolent) of the child. This curious situation is heightened by the dictum which indicates that a *wise son makes a glad father while a foolish son is the heaviness of his mother*. Verily, a foolish son is a grief to his father and bitterness to her that procreated him.

In such an enigmatic situation, it is only *Dike Omenka, Chiokike* – the God of creation who predetermines the seemingly mirage destiny of every child right from the womb, knows what every child would be; as the wicked are estranged from the womb.

Haply, the birth of ***Nwadinobi*** was an exception, as those who knew the circumstances surrounding his procreation and the innate criminality of his biological father, predicted accurately what he would be; for axiomatically, *ele* (antelope) and her offspring are like siamese twin, eternally adorned and glued in one attire.

Yes! As the viper lives and dies with its venom, so was the fate of *Nwadinobi*, the eponymous villain of this chef d"oeuvre - piece of work

CONTENTS

Phase One

The Prodigy

Phase Two

The Imp

Phase Three

The Sacrilege

Phase Four

The Hydra

Phase Five

The Lamentation

Phase One

Characters

Dikeoha: The Prodigy

Ekechi: Dikeoha"s Wife

Mazi Mkpuruoka Okeosisi: Ekechi"s Father

Ekemma: Ekechi"s Mother

Upere: Dikeoha"s Uncle

Nwanyiorie: Ekechi"s younger sister

Okoroigwe: Ekechi"s younger brother

Nsiko: Dikeoha"s bosom buddy

Nwa-Agboso: Nsiko"s younger brother

Mazi Isu: Palm wine taper

Youngsters: Fetchers of water

Ebubedike: Upere"s youngest lad

Mazi Osueke Abalidiegwu: Nwadinobi"s biological poppa

Umunna: Kinsmen

Nwadinobi: The bastard

Phase Two

Characters

Dikeoha: The head of a family

Ekechi: Dikeoha"s wife

Nwadinobi: The anathema

Kawawa (Male): }

Adaku (Female): } Dikeoha"s biological offsprings

Ugwumba(Male): }

Uluaku (Female): }

Akunobi: A victim of Nwadinobi"s criminality

Nwanyiure: Whose daughter was raped by Nwadinobi

Anoka: His properties were stolen by Nwadinobi and his gang of marauders

The messengers (Ugwu, Uzo and Okochi): Brought message to Dikeoha about Nwadinobi"s broken arm at the wrestling arena.

Anufe: The great wrestler

Dibia Ngborogwu: The native doctor that treated Nwadinobi"s fractured arm

Nwokenkwo Anowi: The great palm wine taper

Nmabaraego: Nwadinobi"s head wife

Ebebe Akpaka: Nmabaraego"s father

Urubedi: Kawawa"s wife

Okereke: Urubedi"s Father

Dinta: Kawawa"s Chum

Okembe: Informed Ekechi about Ugwumba"s serfdom status in Kumirukiki.

Uwadiegwu: The village scribe

Ugombachukwu: Kawawa"s first son

Nwabeke: White man or people

Umundomi: Womenfolks

Akueze: Ugwumba"s aborted bride

Osisiogu: Akueze"s Father

Ezeudo: The spokesperson for Rumuoma

Nze Kamalu: Rumuogu"s spokesman

Urediya: Akueze"s mother

Okoh: Rumuogu"s provost

Everybody: All those that was present at Akueze"s marital rites

People of Rumuogu: Osisiogu"s Umunna (kinsmen)

People of Rumuoma: Dikeoha's Umunna (kinsmen)

Akubueze: One of the youths from Rumuoma, who were at Akueze"s marital rite

Ibika: The youth leader from Rumuogu

Nze Okeke: Leader of the bride price negotiation team from Rumuogu

Ichie Ezindu: Leader of the bride price negotiation team from Rumuoma

All Members: The entire bride price negotiation team.

Phase Three

Characters

Osuji: Mgbafor"s former fiancé

Mgbafor: Nwadinobi"s second wife

Nwadinobi: Osuji"s bosom friend

Dikeoha: The patriarch

Ekechi: The matriarch

Osisiogu: Ugwumba"s ex-father in-law

Ekwendu: Osisiogu"s son

Umunna: Osisiogu"s kinsmen

Ibu: One of Osisiogu"s kinsmen

Osondu: Osisiogu"s kinsman (who handed over Akueze"s bride price to Nwadinobi)

Uguru: }

Ikoro: } Osisiogu"s kinsmen

Ojii: }

Orji: }

Ebebe: }

Ikemba age grade: Ugwumba"s age group

Obidike: Led the Rumuoma people to the marital rite of Mgbafor

Iwuala: Spokesperson for the people of Rumuabali

Kawawa: The soldier

Ugwumba: The fashion designer

Uzoma: Ugwumba"s childhood friend and age mate

Ukandu: Ikemba age grade"s spokesman

Amadi: The owner of the fashion house where Ugwumba had a refresher course

Okonkwo: The thrift merchant

Ugoeze: Ugwumba"s wife

Ufere Toti: Rumuoma"s Town crier

Ezeudo: The head of Ndichie

Ndichie: The Elders.

Phase Four

Characters

Nwadinobi: The black widow

Egwuonwu: The benevolent witch doctor (priest) of Utaka

Okaome: The malevolent chief priest of *Agbala Ogbunabali*

Nneji: The hunter

Ndichie: The Elders

Ekechi: Dikeoha"s widow

Ezeudo: Leader of the elders.

Kawawa: The Warrant Officer.

D.P.O. Divisional Police Officer

Sergeant Isigwuzo:} Arrested Nwadinobi

Corporal Ala-Agboso}

The Town Crier: Announces the death of Ekechi

Ugwumba: Sojourned in Ivory Coast

Obidike: The mouthpiece of the people of Rumuoma after the demise of Ezeudo

Ekurume: Ezeudo"s age mate

Okagbue: The chief priest of *Agbala ogbu nwata mgbe ñdu diya utó*

Osama: Nwadinobi"s son

Mbazuigwe: The adroit cutter of trees (tree feller)

Nduka: Ugwumba"s kinsman

Umunna: Kinsmen

Phase Five

Characters

Ugwumba: The stoic

Chibuike: Ugwumba"s eldest lad

Okpuzu: The builder, who rebuilt Ugwumba"s demolished house

Ihueze: Ugwumba"s son

Obidike: Rumuoma"s mouthpiece

Nwadinobi: The evil genius

Osama: The heir-apparent to Nwadinobi"s evil network

Azika: Nwadinobi"s daughter

Odikazi: Kawawa"s son

Visitors: Those who came to sympathize with Nwadinobi and Nmabaraego on their sick bed.

Ufu: One of the visitors

Okengwu: Nwadinobi"s in-law

Ichie Anosike: Rumuishi"s mouthpiece.

Umunna: Kinsmen

Nwakaibeya: One of the elders of Rumuishi.

Iteigwe: Osama"s friend

PHASE ONE
The Prodigy

PROLOGUE

In the dusty, remote village of Rumuoma in the Igbo hinterland, across the East of River Niger, lived a prodigy called Dikeoha.

Dikeoha was an orphan, having lost his parents and only brother at a very tender age. Determined to survive, he took to the family trade of herbal healing at that tender age, walking and trekking thousands of miles in the dispensation of his craft. Indeed, the god of healing was with him. He was able to give succour to „seemingly" barren women. One could refer to him as a traditional gynecologist. His sobriquet rings a bell in the ears of those who at one time or the other interacted with him.

Dikeoha was a man of peace and justice. In the course of his herbal medical practice, it was said that, after preparing the medicine, he would ask his client to pay before dispensing the drug; if she promised to pay him in future, he would consume his drug and beckon on her to invite him whenever she is ready for payment. This was not an act of wickedness. It was all because he detests quarrelling with anyone because of mere debt. Suffice it to say that, years back our people in the Eastern part of Nigeria preferred to save money for thrift business to paying for drugs to cure their ailments. To him, you either choose between saving for thrift at the detriment of your health and paying for drugs and saving your life from attack from diseases.

More importantly, Dikeoha was left with a lot of farmlands, being the only surviving child. As a result of greed, his kinsmen wished him death, so that they could take over the lands. However, God"s hand was on his side. Having grown to manhood, after the initiation of *Iwa-akwa* (tying cloth ceremony) and *Igbu-ichi*, he began to solicit for a life partner.

The quest for a better half took him to a far village called Rumuodara, across the dreaded Aham and Iyiocha Rivers. He met and got entangled with a comely damsel called *Ekechi*. Coincidentally, the mother of the nubile was his former patient. The introduction and other negotiations began.

Determined to frustrate Dikeoha and prevent him from having his own children, who will inherit his possessions, especially farmlands, one of his trusted kinsmen called *Upere* began a campaign of calumny.

Act One

Scene 1

Dikeoha: [on the road to Rumuekpe market, soliciting to win Ekechi"s hand in marriage.] Excuse me, comely damsel, may I know you?

Ekechi: [pretending not to have heard the question, continuing her journey.]

Dikeoha: [in the mood of a desperado, overtook Ekechi and reiterated his first query, waiting for an answer.] Please, may I know you?

Ekechi: [at this juncture, make a pause while covering her face shyly with her left hand and at the same time using her feet (big toe) to sketch incomprehensible figures on the ground. Dikeoha was, however, kept in suspense.]

Dikeoha: [having understood that, the damsel (probably a virgin) was shy to talk to a man in the open. He then followed her, until they got to an *'apiam way'* – narrow track. It was at this point that Dikeoha employed his sonorous voice into action. He reiterated his plea again for the third time.] *Biko* (please) I would like to know you.

Ekechi: [inwardly overwhelmed by Dikeoha"s physique and voice, but still pretending, rhetorically demanded why Dikeoha was interested to know her.] Thus, why do
you want to know me, who are you by the way?

Dikeoha: Sorry my dear, I would have introduced myself to you before my enquiries, however, it was your beauty that carried me away.

Ekechi: Please, stop flattering me; tell me who you are.

Dikeoha: I"m the beloved son of *Mazi Ebekuodike* of Rumuoma. My father was an itinerant herbal doctor of varied diseases, especially for women searching for the fruit of the womb - children. Worthy, I took over from my father when he died some years back.

Ekechi: [Cut in.] Oh! Oh!! Oh!!! Are you Dikeoha, the herbal doctor with divine endowment?

Dikeoha: Do you know me?

Ekechi: Not really, but my parents, especially my mother, do talk about a prodigy called Dikeoha from Rumuoma, who aided her so many times to get pregnant via his herbal medicine. I wonder if you are actually the one.

Dikeoha: Who are your parents and where do they come from?

Ekechi: My father"s name is *Mazi Mkpuruoka Okeosisi* while my mother"s name is *Ekemma.* We are from Rumuodara, the village across the dreaded Aham and Iyiocha Rivers.

Dikeoha: You see, the human race is just one. Just imagine the divine intervention of providence. My dear, your family is just like my mine.Your home is my home. Your parents and I are in a palsy-walsy relationship.

Ekechi: [gradually gaining confidence, still insisting to know if this Dikeoha was actually the one depicted to her by her mother.] Thus, are you the Dikeoha talked about by my parents?

Dikeoha: I"m your mother"s doctor. Before it escapes my memory, what is your name?

Ekechi: [while beaming with smiles.] My name is Ekechi.

Dikeoha: What a lovely name, are you the first or second daughter? It"s been a longtime, since I visited your home and you are all grown-ups now.

Ekechi: I"m the first daughter.

Dikeoha: Hmmn, Please, take this *anu-nchi* (cutting-grass or bush meat) to your parents; tell them that it came from Dikeoha, their family doctor cum friend. As for you, take this shekel as a token, I will see you on the next *eké* market day. Greet your parents for me.

Ekechi: [full of joy, amiably thanked Dikeoha and departed.] Thank you very much, Nnanyi.

Dikeoha: [while on his way home, shouted.] Eureka! [The aura of his chat with Ekechi overshadowed his sense of rationality to the extent that he injured himself, when he unknowingly crashed into a tree before him.]

Ekechi: [with the hindsight of clairvoyance, was also on her way home reminiscing about her discussion with Dikeoha, whom she saw as her dreamed hubby.]

Dikeoha: [Eventually, got home and treated his wound, albeit, stoically pretended not to be feeling the pains, for love's sake. He began to meditate on his would-be encounter with Ekechi, the next *eké* market day. He, however, kept all these to himself.]

Scene 2

Ekechi: [got home at last and told her parents, her encounter with Dikeoha.] *Ehen*! Papa and mama, please come, I have something for you.

Mkpuruoka and Ekemma: [simultaneously] we are coming oh, (as they rushed to the parlour) our daughter, here we are.

Ekechi:[hilariously] I saw Dikeoha, the herbal doctor and he gave me this *anu-nchi* – cutting grass *(bushmeat)* to give to you. He said that you are family friends.

Mkpuruoka and Ekemma: Oh! Oh! Chei! Dikeoha, that good man remembered us today! God is with him. His healings are an act of God. He is so humble that any parent would cherish having him as an in-law. He is down to earth. God will give him a good wife, but we still wonder why he is still single. No woman that knows him would refuse to accept his proposal for marriage.

Mkpuruoka: [left mother and daughter behind.] Hmmn, Ekemma, let me go and see my yam farm.

Ekemma: Okay, nnanyi. You see my daughter; Dikeoha is the herbal doctor I was telling you about, that aided me in procreation, through his afflatus or esoteric herbal medicine.

Ekechi: [being tacit, acknowledged the qualities of Dikeoha as enumerated by her parents, rhetorically inquired thus.] So he is a good man and our family friend too? Why is it that, he seldom visits us?

Ekemma: My daughter, you know Dikeoha is as busy as an ant; he has an avalanche of clients that he attends to.

Ekechi: He must be a wealthy man, synchronizing his multitude of clients.

Ekemma: My daughter, life is not all about wealth. Actually, I don"t know the material worth of Dikeoha, but I think he is comfortable. Dikeoha is not a greedy fellow. He charges his clients paltry fees. His effort is more or less a humanitarian vocation. That is the reason why God should multiply whatever he laid his hands on.

Ekechi: Mama, what type of soup are we going to prepare tonight?

Ekemma: Thank you my daughter for that question. You see, with the *„anu-nchi'* given to us by Dikeoha, I would suggest we prepare *Ofe egusi* with *ugu* and *ukazi* leaves. I am sure your father will appreciate the delicacy; hence, *Ofe Egusi* with *ugu* and *ukazi* leaves taken with *nri ji* (pounded yam) is his best bet. It was this combination that lured me to him. A man"s heart is with his stomach. The instant, you sumptuously satisfy the stomach, his heart is at the matrix of your palm.

Ekechi: Okay, mama let me start the preparations before it"s too late.

Ekemma: *O ya nwam nwanyi bido ósósó* (okay my daughter start quickly).

Ekemma and Ekechi: [Finished cooking.]

Ekemma: [having dished out the food in rations, beckon the children to serve their father first before collecting their own ration.]

Mkpuruoka: [while eating with his wife, commended her for a work well-done.] Che…e, this is one of the delicious meals that lured you to me in our youthful days. I will rarely forget your sumptuous meals. I know *Chiokike* (god of creation) endows you with a cookery gift (there was general laughter).

Mkpuruoka: [after the meal, went to his temple to pray to his *chi* to safeguard him and his household to see the next day.] *Chiokike*! I bring you kola nut, alligator pepper and gin, take these for your protection and guidance over my family. Protect us to see the next sunlight. Hmmm, he who said that we will not live, will also not see the next sunrise. Ours is, live and let live.

All the children: [bade their parents good night and went to sleep on raffia-made beds and mats on top.]

Scene 3

Life continues until the next *eke* market day.

Dikeoha: [Soliloquizing.] Today is my date with Ekechi, but I'm yet to tell her about my feelings for her. *Chei*, how do I go about it today? Should I tell her that I like her or love her or that I want to marry her or should I ask her for friendship? Hmm, I don"t want to make a mistake o. Okay, I will buy some gift items for her and work on her psychology, thereafter, I will know what to say.

Ekechi: [On her way to the market, soliloquizing.] *Chei*, how I wish Dikeoha will be so kind enough to tell me that he wants to marry me. He is my ideal man and *Chiokike* will grant my heart's desire.

Dikeoha: [got to the market early and purchased some gift items. The instant he saw Ekechi in the Rumuekpe market, he dodged her and moved towards the bush track to lay ambush for her on her way home.]

Ekechi: [on her way home was contemplating why Dikeoha did not come to the market that day.] Is Dikeoha hale and hearty? What is wrong with him? Did he actually remember today"s date? Maybe he is taking care of an emergency situation.

Dikeoha: [as Ekechi was soliloquizing, emerged from an adjacent bush track.] Hello, beautiful girl! How are you and your household? I hope all is well?

Ekechi: [striving to suppress her hilarity.] We are okay Nnanyi. But where are you coming from?

Dikeoha: Hmm, I am coming from the market.

Ekechi: [cut in.] But, I searched for you in the market without seeing you. Where were you hiding?

Dikeoha: Why should I hide? As you know, *a golden fish has no hiding place*. I bought these gift items for you, right from the market. O ya, take them, they are for you.

Ekechi: I"m sorry, Nnanyi for querying you; I would have believed you, if not for curiosity. But for the gift items, keep them, I will not take.

Dikeoha: Why won"t you accept a gift from a sincere heart?

Ekechi: You see, my parents will chop off my head, if they got to know about the gift items. They admonished us not to accept gifts of any kind from men, especially those who are not our betrothed.

Dikeoha: [exploiting his inherent ethos pressurized her to accept the gift items, thus.] Ekechi, please take these gift items from a loving and sincere heart, instead, conceal them where your parents will not see them, until when the time is ripe.

Ekechi: [sharply inquired.] What do you mean by „when the time is ripe?"

Dikeoha: Please, accept the items first, and then I will be in the right position to explicate the teaser.

Ekechi: Em! Em!! Okay, I will accept, only if you will answer my question o, because I"m lost.

Dikeoha: My dear, there is always a silver lining in the skies and a light at the end of the tunnel.

Ekechi: Nnanyi, you should know that I'm not mature enough to apprehend your idiomatic expressions. I"m always at a loss whenever you talk.

Dikeoha: Hmm, my love, there is no need to pinch a wrapped material, when you know that you can unwrap the same at the appropriate time. As you must have heard, kolanut and snuff (powdered tobacco) stay long in the mouth of those that appreciate their value.

Ekechi: Nnanyi, you are keeping me in suspense, how do you expect me to understand these aphorisms? Please answer my questions to my own understanding. If not, I will not accept the items o.

Dikeoha: Okay, Ekechi, listen to me now, *Chiokike* is my witness, right from the first day I set my eyes on you, my personal „*chi*" – guardian angel revealed to me that you are my wife. Yes, you are my dreamed heartthrob and little angel. I want you to be the mother of my children. Will you marry me?

Ekechi: [inwardly full of joy.] You know that, your query is not easy to comeby and as such would not receive an instant response. Please, you should give me time to sleep over it. I hope to give you an answer in the next two *eke*-market days.

Dikeoha: [being happy that she accepted the gift items.] Thanks for your patience and understanding. Please, my love, consider my request with a kind heart. Em! Em!! I"m too young to have cardiac arrest. Greet your parents for me. Keep fit, until then, adieu.

Scene 4

On the second eké market day, Dikeoha and Ekechi met at their usual rendezvous.

Dikeoha: [in deep thought, because of anxiety.] Hmm! Ekechi my dear, how are you and members of your household?

Ekechi: Em! Em!! Nnanyi everybody was hale and hearty when I left home. How about you and your vocation, I hope all is well?

Dikeoha: As you can see, I"m fine. Em! Em!! Ekechi, my dear, what is the result of my Cambridge exam? Did I pass?

Ekechi: [beaming with broad smiles.] Nnanyi, you really dealt with the exam questions excellently. Congratulations.

Dikeoha: [with a deep sigh of relief, enthused.] Oh, my beloved, I deeply appreciate your consideration. I will never disappoint you. I"m making a vow that you will never regret this priceless decision. Come and embrace me, my gold dust jewel. You see, by the turn of the next eight *afor* market day, I will come and see your parents as tradition would demand.

Ekechi: [still in Dikeoha"s arms.] Nnanyi, you have spoken well, I pray this will come to pass; I don"t want to be far away from you.

Dikeoha: My dear, I feel the same way as you, but our tradition should be followed religiously; taking a wife is not like buying a goat in the market. The gradual process being followed in marriage rites is the beauty of marriage.

Ekechi: Nnanyi, you are so humane and understanding that, I feel like telling you all about myself. Em! Em!! Before I forget that I"m still under my parents" tutelage, let me be going. Nnanyi, I will see you on the next *eke* market day. Good bye.

Dikeoha: Hmmn, it"s too hard to let you go, but the time is up. See you on the appointed day, cheerio.

Scene 5

Dikeoha: [went home and told one of his seemingly trusted uncles, Upere.] Nnanyi Upere, I have seen a girl that I would like to marry. Em, em, being an orphan, I"m imploring you to fill my parental lacuna.

Upere: [unctuously, as being supportive, queried thus.] Where is the nubile from, and from which family?

Dikeoha: She hails from Rumuodara, the village across the dreaded Aham and Iyiocha Rivers. She is the first daughter of Mazi Mkpuruoka Okeosisi, the great farmer, the Ezeji of our time.

Upere: [wondering in his mind, how Dikeoha, an orphan was able to win the love of such a girl, enthused.] Hmmn! Okay, when are you commencing the traditional marriage rite?

Dikeoha: Nnanyi, I will take you there first, to see things for yourself before the introduction proper.

Upere: When are we going?

Dikeoha: I hope the next *eké* market day will be okay for you?

Upere: Yes, let"s go on that day.

Scene 6

On the D-day, Dikeoha and Upere began their journey to Rumuodara and arrived after a long trek.

Dikeoha and Upere: [knocking at Mazi Mkpuruoka"s door.] Koi! Koi!! Who is here?

Nwanyi Orie: [Ekechi"s younger sister came out to open the door. She welcomes the visitors, thus.] *Unu abiala? Nnonu* (Have you come? Welcome.)

The visitor: [responded thus.] *Iyaa, nwa oma* (yes, good child)

Nwanyi Orie: [led them in, and they met with her parents.] Nnanyi, come in, my parents are here.

The visitors: Okay, our daughter.

Mkpuruoka and Ekemma: [on sighting the strangers, stood up to receive them.] Our visitors, you are welcome. How about your household? We hope all is well?

The visitors: We are okay, but for our household, they were hale and hearty by the time we left home.

Mkpuruoka: [having sent for kola nut, he presented the same to the visitors.] My people, this is kola nut.

The visitors: [tacitly telling Mkpuruoka to pray over the kola nut, enthused.] Em! Em!! We have seen it, thank you very much; let the king"s kola nut remain with him.

Mkpuruoka: [Prayed over the kola nut, thus.] *Chiokike* (God of creation), this is kola nut, we are saying that he who brings kola nut brings life and he who eats it, eats life. Kola nut is a symbol of love and brotherliness in our land and as such, he who comes to your house with evil intention(s), hunchback shall not fail to accompany him on his way home and vice versa. Hmm, we are beckoning on you to bless this kola nut and those that will eat it, so that good health, procreation, wealth and long life shall be our portion here on earth, *iséé*...

The visitors: *Iséé,* you have prayed well.

Mkpuruoka: [called one of his sons, thus.] Okoroigwe, come over here.

Okoroigwe: Nnanyi, here I"m.

Mkpuruoka: Okoroigwe, my son, break this kola nut and serve us, after this, go to the shade beside the yam barn, bring the palm wine in the big keg here.

Okoroigwe: [after some minutes.] Nnanyi, this is the palm wine.

Mkpuruoka: You have done well, my son. Now serve us as tradition would demand.

Okoroigwe: [served his father first before others as tradition would demand, since he is the host.] Nnanyi, this is yours.

The visitors: Mazi Mkpuruoka, you have done very well, we appreciate your kola nut and *nkwu-elu* (Palm wine).

Mkpuruoka: [cut in.] Ekemma! Ekemma!!

Ekemma: Oee! Nnanyi, I"m coming.

Mkpuruoka: [confidentially asked her.] Have you finished preparing the *egusi soup* and *pounded yam*?

Ekemma: Nnanyi, the food will be ready in a jiffy.

Mkpuruoka: Please, my dear, hasten up, as you know, these people came from a far distance.

Ekemma: [while leaving.] Okay, Nnanyi, I have heard you.

Mkpuruoka: [talking to the visitors.] Please, sorry for the hitch in communication. I was striving to sort-out one or two things with my wife.

The visitors: Don"t bother yourself, we understand and appreciate your gold dust concern.

Dikeoha: [introducing Upere to their host.] Mazi Mkpuruoka, this man here (pointing at Upere) is my uncle.

Upere: Mazi, *ñno*, I greet you. My nephew has told me a lot about you, that is why I decided to accompany him to your abode.

Mkpuruoka: Em! Upere, you have done well, it is a sign of good brotherliness. I know that with a personality like you on Dikeoha"s side, he will not derail or go astray. Dikeoha is a good family friend of ours.

Upere: [unctuously.] Thank you Mazi for the compliments, I know the relationship has also extended to me.

Mkpuruoka: That is true; hence, you are of Dikeoha"s lineage.

Ekechi: [coming back from the stream, greeted the visitors before putting down the water pot on her head.] *Nnanyi, unu abiala, ñnónu* (my elders, have you come? Welldone).

The visitors: Thank you beautiful girl.

Dikeoha: [whispering to Upere.] Nnanyi, this is the comely damsel I told you about.

Upere: [nodding his head like an agama lizard.] Okay.

Ekechi: [came in some minutes later with the food to serve the visitors.] Nnanyi, this is your meal.

Mkpuruoka: [went over to the visitors" table and tasted the food as tradition would demand to avoid any suspicion of food poisoning.] My people, you can now enjoy your meal.

The visitors: [fed to their satisfaction, thanked their host.] Mazi and Ekemma, you have done well, thank you for the hospitality. Em, Ekemma, you deserve an award for your cookery prowess, the soup is sumptuous, no wonder your husband is like the eucalyptus tree, always evergreen. Mazi, you are a lucky man.

Dikeoha: [unctuously but jokingly.] Em, I hope your daughters will follow your footprint?

Ekemma: [beaming with smiles.] Oh, yes, my daughters cook very well, even Ekechi cooks better than me.

Dikeoha: [this attribute of Ekechi, gladdened his heart and his soul rejoices) Eeh! Hmm! So Ekechi can cook very well? Maybe this trait is in your family.

Ekemma: [still beaming with smiles.] Yes, it is a divine gift from *Chiokike*. Nnanyi, let me go and rearrange my utensils (she left)

Mkpuruoka: My people, I must confess to you, this woman is specially designed for me by *Chiokike,* I really thank God for this gesture. You know a virtuous wife is hard to find, a man"s jewelry is his wife. What I"m saying is that, a man"s worth in public depends on his wife"s demeanour. She is indeed my missing rib.

The visitors: Mazi, you are indeed blessed with a good wife and amiable children, needless to say that, we envy you.

Mkpuruoka: Thanks for your peerless compliments.

The visitors: Em, Mazi, we have to be on our way now, as you know, we have a long way to go. Greet your wife and children on our behalf.

Mkpuruoka: [while escorting them.] Thank you very much, for your visit; I highly appreciate your concern over my household. I will try and return your visit one of these days. I wish you journey mercies.

The Visitors: Mazi, you have done well and spoken well too, thank you once again, may our ancestors, protect your entire household. Amen. We will be expecting your return visit as promised. *Chiokike* will be with you.

Mkpuruoka: [responding.] *iséé o, ya gazie*, let it be well. Keep fit and bye for now. (They departed from each other).

Upere: [while on their way home, was contemplating in his mind how Dikeoha whom he wished dead, in order to acquire all his landed properties left for him by his late parents will now be talking of getting married very soon. He was carried away by thought to the extent that Dikeoha noticed his ambiance.]

Dikeoha: Nnanyi Upere, are you okay? I can see that you are not concentrating on our discussion. Is anything the matter?

Upere: [in a hocus-pocus craft.] Em! Em!! I"m okay, it's just that I was reflecting on the lavish entertainment accorded us by Mazi Mkpuruoka and indeed the journey ahead, as you know, I have to attend to my palm trees for wine production this evening.

Dikeoha: Nnanyi, don"t worry, we will soon reach home.

Upere: [when they got home, still contemplating in his mind, managed to say goodbye.] Dikeoha thank God, we have finally gotten home. Goodbye, I hope to see you later in the day or rather tomorrow because after attending to my palm trees, I have to relax my nerves because I"m groggy.

Dikeoha: Okay, Nnanyi, you have done well. God bless you for your brotherly concern. I will see you tomorrow, goodnight. (They departed, each man to his tent)

Scene 7

Dikeoha: [the next day went to his chum, Nsiko - the crab and beckoned him to escort him to his would-be in-law"s place, the next *afor* market day.] Nsiko, as I was saying, you have to accompany me to my heartthrob"s place on the next afor.

Nsiko: Hmm, Dikeoha, I hope you shined your eyes very well before choosing this girl of yours? As you know very well, our mates will not take it kindly with you, if your would-be wife is not a diamond, after all these years of bachelorhood.

Dikeoha: [jokingly.] My friend, just accompany me, my wife is not for my age grade but for me. I would admonish you to keep your cool until you see her, there and then; you will realize that I"m not „the beautiful eagle that consumes toads". I always go for the best. Nsiko, you can trust me for that.

Nsiko: [being so funny and witty.] You are now bragging; let it not be the other way round o. If she is not the sort of girl that befits a member of our age grade, I will desert you there and return home. Em! Em!! I hope you have bought the traditional hot drink for the girl"s father, as tradition would demand?

Dikeoha: Nsiko, my friend, as I said earlier on, just keep your cool, all is well. You see, I did not grow into manhood with inherent cowardice. I"m from the warrior family, a lion does not give birth to a weakling. Have you forgotten that my middle name is „tradition"? I have purchased all that is needed for our journey, the next *afor* market day.

Nsiko: Dikeoha, if I may ask, why not shift this all important journey to *eké* market day, so that we can enjoy oil bean (ugba) with stockfish (okporoko) and tapioca bought from the market. As you know very well, meals prepared on *eké* market day are always special.

Dikeoha: *Chei,* you see, when I told you that my middle name is „tradition", you laughed at me. Are you not aware that issues relating to the marriage of a spinster are not carried out on *eké* market day? It is also a taboo in the larger Igbo race. Afor-ukwu market day is the best bet.

Nsiko: [being jocose.] Okay o, Mr. Custodian of Igbo tradition, I have heard you. Let"s go and visit Ekeanyanwu"s palm wine joint at least let's take some bottles for the day.

Dikeoha: Nsiko, are you in a wonderland? Have you forgotten that I'm not used to such joints? I prefer buying a keg of palm wine and drinking to my satisfaction here to going to that public place.

Nsiko: Once again, you have made another valid point. Why not send Nwa-agboso
to go and fetch a keg for us immediately. At least let"s talk over it while relaxing our nerves after the stressfulness of the day.

Dikeoha: [calling Nwa-agboso.] Nwa-agboso! Nwa-agboso!! Nwa-agboso!!! Where is this boy? Nsiko, where is your brother?

Nwa-agboso: [suddenly appeared.] Nnanyi, here I"m.

Nsiko: Nwa-agboso, why did you refuse to answer the call?

Nwa-agboso: Nnanyi, I was chewing hard meat, when I heard the call, so I decided to rush to you, instead of opening my mouth to answer which was not possible instantly.

Dikeoha: Now, go to Mazi Isu"s house, tell him that, I said, he should give you one big keg of fresh palm wine *„nkwu elu'*. Tell him also that I will see him tomorrow for payment.

Nwa-agboso: Okay, Nnanyi, (he went and brought the palm wine as ordered).

Dikeoha: [tasted the wine and exclaimed.] This wine is original, not those sold at public joints after being mixed with Imo river. Nsiko, taste it, I know that, from today henceforth you will not drink palm wine from any other taper, except that of Mazi Isu. You see, this wine will add meaning to your life.

Nsiko: [before tasting the wine, enthused.] Hei, Mr Advert manager, please, allow me to taste the wine and make my own comment; you can only speak for yourself, afterall, you ordered the palm wine. It‟s not surprising seeing you exerting all your energy extolling the taper and the wine.

Dikeoha: My dear, I withdrew my comments; but just have a sip of the wine.

Nsiko: [while tasting the wine.] Dikeoha, I have known you for a long time as a real gent with taste, I was merely trying to pull your legs. My friend, this is more than ordinary palm wine. Are you sure that this wine is not an affiliate to the miraculous wine of Nazareth? This is the type of wine meant for people like us, who are on the verge of taking a wife. Yes, the instant we knew our wives, just one touch, it would click.

Dikeoha: Yes, you have said it all. Hm, lest I forgot, how about Chioke, your grandfather?

Nsiko: He is still battling with geriatrics.

Dikeoha: [they continued drinking, till evening when Dikeoha begged to leave in order to attend to other pressing issues at home.] Nsiko, I beg to leave now, please don‟t forget our date. I pray, *Chiokike* will keep us hale and hearty till that day. Goodbye.

Nsiko: Dikeoha, why not stay for some time? Don‟t you know that, your desertion will keep me in solitude?

Dikeoha: Nsiko, loneliness is one of the reasons why *Chiokike* created the first woman called Ahudo for the first man called Ikenga. This is the reason why you should get a wife for yourself.

Nsiko:[mockingly.] Ugh! Mr. Husband, thank you for the citation. If I may ask, are you not in the same turbulent boat with me? Afterall, you have not even gone for the marital introduction. However, after our journey to your would-be in-law‟s abode, I will take you to my heartthrob for assessment.

Dikeoha: My friend! Now, you are talking sense. As you may be aware, an aphorism has it that, if the first son does not behave like a batty fellow, his parents wouldn"t realize that he had matured enough to have a wife. They will still be seeing him as a toddler.

Nsiko: Dikeoha, I really appreciate your concern, you are a very good friend. I have to leave you now, to go.

Dikeoha: Nsiko, as you know, what affects you also affects me. Let me say once again, goodbye and God bless.

Nsiko: [while escorting Dikeoha, queried.] Dikeoha, have you told your fiancée „Ekechi" about our visit?

Dikeoha: My dear, I have not done that yet, but I hope to apprise her on this forthcoming *eké* market day. Hmmn, now that we are at this big Iroko tree adjacent to Mbara, I"m almost at home; you can go back and clear the keg and wine cups.

Nsiko: Thank you for your understanding, bye, bye.

Scene 8

Nsiko: [being a trusted and witty friend came out on time on the D-day.] Ol" boy, are you still preparing, don"t you know that today is your bonafide „first" date?

Dikeoha: Nsiko my friend, you are welcome. Please don"t mind me. I have been searching fruitlessly for the best attire to put on for the journey. I"m yet to decide on the one to wear.

Nsiko: My friend, you are funny, just pick one of those clothes, let"s set out for the journey, as you are aware, we have a long way to go including the passage of the dreaded Aham River which is infested with long mouthed *Aguiyi* - crocodiles. Em! Em!! Your clothes have nothing to do with your acceptability, hence your would-be in-laws know you before now.

Dikeoha: [picked one of the clothes as admonished by Nsiko, who praised the outfits.] Nsiko, let"s proceed; you will be my gas bag there o. I know you are good at rhetorics.

Nsiko: [boasting.] Who does not know that oratory is my middle name? Have you ever seen or heard of any girl that turned me down? I"m any lady"s beau.

Dikeoha: Hei, listen, you may be any lady"s fancy man but not for my Ekechi. She is God sent, she is my missing rib and she has come to fill the yawning gap, just to make me a complete man. I guess you know exactly what I"m talking about.

Nsiko: [unctuously.] I don"t know what you are talking about. Can you elaborate further?

Dikeoha: You see, any man who is not married and he is not a priest is not complete because the rib taken from him by *Chiokike* to form the woman is still missing.

Nsiko: [while on their journey.] My dear, you are so infatuated with this „queen" of yours. I really envy you o. How I wish my greed for women will allow me to settle down with this present girl of mine.

Dikeoha: Don"t worry. Our ancestors are considering your request; perhaps, after today"s journey, a new spirit of faithfulness will overcome your being, and you will settle down with your current heartthrob.

Nsiko: [while in the village of Rumuodara.] Dikeoha, where is the family? We are already in Rumuodara.

Dikeoha: It"s just after the next six buildings.

Nsiko: My dear, why did you decide to go this far in search of a wife, does it mean that there are no beautiful damsels in the neighbouring villages of Rumuosochie, Rumuokwe, Rumunachi, Rumuofia and Rumunia?

Dikeoha: Nsiko, marriage is an esoteric institution, only those with spiritual eyes can see and understand what entails therein. Marriage is always caused by providence, and such cause is beyond our curb. For you to have a peaceful marriage life, allow *Chiokike* to provide a wife for you, no matter where she emanates from. As our people say, *Nwanyi enweghi obodo. Obodo di ya bu obodo ya* (a woman does not have a community; her husband"s community is equally hers).

Nsiko: I can now appreciate your position very well; you are indeed a man of wisdom. I thank God we are friends.

Dikeoha: Nsiko, this is our destination, let me knock at the door (knocking) koi, koi!! Who is here?

Ekechi: [having knowledge of the visit, came out to open the door.] You are welcome, *ñnonu.*

Dikeoha: Where are your parents?

Ekechi: Please have your seats and let me go and look for my father, he didn"t go far. My mother went to visit her sick friend at the next two buildings.

Dikeoha: Nsiko, please sit down.

Ekechi: [went out to call her parents.] Papa, some people are waiting for you at home.

Mkpuruoka: Who are they?

Ekechi: I only recognized one of them, Nnanyi Dikeoha, but I have not seen the other person before.

Mkpuruoka: [rushed home and greeted the visitors.] My people, you are welcome, „*ñnonu*".

Ekemma: [came in after the presentation of kola nut and greeted the visitors and went in to give a directive to *Nwanyiorie* to start preparing food for the visitors.] *Ndi obia anyi, unu abiala, ñnonu* (our visitors have you come. Well done)

Dikeoha: [after all entreaties, introduced Nsiko (the crab) to his would-be in-laws.] Mazi Mkpuruoka, this is my bosom friend, his name is Nsiko.

Mkpuruoka: [smiled amusingly at the name, however welcomed Nsiko, while discussions continued] Nsiko you"re welcomed to my humble abode.

Dikeoha: [after the meal, whispered to Nsiko to introduce their mission to Mazi Mkpuruoka.]

Nsiko: [cleared his throat.] *Mazi imela oji, ma nyekwe anyi nri, Chukwu gozie gi* (Mazi you have given us kola nut and foods, God bless you). Em! Em!! On behalf of my chum, Dikeoha, I present these grog and kola nuts to you. As the saying goes, a frog does not run in daylight for the fun of it. If she is not pursuing prey, a predator is pursuing her. That"s by the way. Mazi, we saw a beautiful flower in your house and long to pluck the same.

Mkpuruoka: [as if taken aback, thanked Nsiko for his oratory prowess, but begged to know who the symbolic flower is.] Nsiko my son, you have spoken well, but may I know the particular flower you are talking about here, hence, I have about four symbolic flowers in my house.

Nsiko: Mazi, your grey hair is that of wisdom, you have once again displayed the parenthood trait in you. You are an elder to be emulated by us youngsters, em, em the beautiful and adorable flower, we are talking about here, is christened Ekechi.

Mukpuruoka: [calling on Ekechi.] Ekechi! Ekechi!!

Ekechi: Oeeh, papa, I"m coming. Here I"m.

Mkpuruoka: Ekechi my daughter, these men said that they came here because of you. If I may ask, do you know any of them?

Ekechi: [pointing at Dikeoha.] Yes, papa, I know this one.

Mkpuruoka: Are you saying that we should accept their token?

Ekechi: Yes, Papa.

Mkpuruoka: Okay, you can go.

Ekechi: [who had hitherto apprised her mother, who in turn informed her father, was beaming with smiles while deserting the scene.] Thank you papa.

Dikeoha and Nsiko: [after the brief introduction, begged to leave and promised to come again in the near future for proper introduction and other marriage rites.] Nnanyi, we must be on our way home right now for the journey is far, we hope to return again soon.

Mkpuruoka: [bade them goodbye.] My would-be in-laws, I wish you journey mercies, may our *chi* guide you to your destination without hitches, *iséé.*

Dikeoha and Nsiko: [as they were leaving, thanked Mazi Mkpuruoka.] Thank you very much, Mazi. *Chiokike* will also protect you and your ménage from every evil intention, *iséé.*

Scene 9

Dikeoha: [after the journey, went to see Upere.] Nnanyi Upere, greetings to you. I went to my in-laws place with my chum, Nsiko. We went to acquaint ourselves with Ekechi‟s parents as custom would demand in order to avoid embarrassment in the event of their knowing about our relationship from outside.

Upere: [pretending to be happy with Dikeoha‟s marriage plans.] Hmmn, so you went there and they accepted your proposal? You must be a lucky man o. I wish you godspeed. Em! Em!! When are we going for the introduction proper?

Dikeoha: Nnanyi, I think we have to put our heads together and map out strategies for the pursuance of the marriage rites. I‟m banking on your wealth of experience on this matter.

Upere: Dikeoha, you ought to know that, I‟m just like your father. I will do anything within my powers to see that you succeed in this entire important mission.

Dikeoha: Thank you for your encouragement, Nnanyi with you on my side, all will be well. Our people used to say that a man‟s *umunna* is his backbone as well as his backache.

Upere: [contemplating on the strategy to scuttle Dikeoha‟s marriage plans, but unctuously showcasing support.] Em! Em!! Dikeoha, my nephew, as far as this marriage is concerned, no *nwanna* (kinsman) will be a backache, in as much as I‟m still alive. Take my word. Your wife will soon come home.

Dikeoha: [eulogized Upere; thanked him again and begged to leave.] Nnanyi Upere, God will protect you; you shall see more days ahead. Em! May I leave now, thanks for your unfettered support. I will see you within the next two *eké* market days, for more deliberations on the marriage rites. Goodbye.

Upere: [as Dikeoha was departing, sighed and began to soliloquize.] Ugh! Go and marry let me see, useless orphan. So you want to marry and have children, who will take over your landed properties? Hmmn, this cannot happen in my sight. You have to die as a bachelor, and my offsprings will in turn inherit your properties… Em! Em!! What should I do now before it"s too late? Okay! That"s it, I have to visit Mazi Mkpuruoka Okeosisi, first thing tomorrow morning, there and then, I will daint your impeccable profile and personality, *anu ofia* (bush meat). My sophistry will nail your coffin tomorrow. Idiot!

Scene 10

Upere: [at Mazi Mkpuruoka"s abode.] Mazi, I thank you for the kola nut and „*nkwu elu*". Hmm, our people do say that, a rabbit does not come out in the daytime for the fun of it. It is also a taboo for an elder to be at home and see a goat on fetters procreating without unfettering her.

Mkpuruoka: Upere, I hope all is well, why all these proverbs?

Upere: Mazi, you are an elder and a well-known personality of our time, em… as an Ezeji (King of yam farmers), you ought to know your worth in the society.

Mkpuruoka: Em! I know my worth in society, please…! What is the message?

Upere: I have come to save you from self-smudging your precious name. You see, that boy, Dikeoha, is a rascal and an orphan; he can"t take good care of your adorable daughter. There is an incurable death spell in his immediate family. I believe you will not like to see your daughter reeling in agony. A stitch in time saves nine.

Mkpuruoka: Thanks for the information. I"m grateful. Our people used to say that it is necessary for elders to be around home, so that little children will not kill lizards for supper. Em! But as the repository of the-out-of-the-way knowledge, why did you accompany him to this place, four *eké* market days ago?

Upere: [cleared his throat.] You see, this boy is as cunning as the tortoise. He didn"t tell me that he was coming to ask for your daughter"s hand in marriage. Em…! Even if he did, I wouldn"t have turned him down openly. I have just come to give you this all important information, for your own consumption only. A word is enough for the wise. He, who rises up from where he was, knows where he is heading to. I beg to leave now, the journey ahead is far.

Mkpuruoka: Thank you once again for your concern. I will give a serious thought to our discussion. Goodbye.

Upere: [while leaving.] Mazi, don"t treat this issue with a kid"s globe; goodbye.

Mkpuruoka: [at home, on his settee,
meditating on the gist devoured to him by Upere.] Chei! Chei!!Hmm.

Ekemma: [came in.] Nnanyi, why are you so solemn, is it well with you? You are not your usual self.

Mkpuruoka: Ekemma, my dear, wonders shall never end. Can you believe that, Upere, Dikeoha"s uncle came here some hours ago and divulged a series of unprinted information about Dikeoha. According to him, Dikeoha is a rascal and an orphan, who cannot take care of our daughter. Above all, he said that there is an incurable death spell on Dikeoha"s family. Summarily, he admonished us not to give out our daughter"s hand in marriage to Dikeoha. Em! I"m just wondering on what line of action to take at this stage, based on the latest revelations.

Ekemma: [being emotionally prejudiced.] Nnanyi, Kia! Kia!! We should apprise Ekechi to forget about Dikeoha and accept any other man of her choice; afterall, Dikeoha is yet to carry out the marriage rites.

Mkpuruoka: Hei, listen woman, I"m a man of honour and if I do not appreciate my status, I will be like the beast that perishes. I must tell you; this information is hard to chew. I consider it with a pinch of salt. Hmm, Upere"s words were smoother than butter but my instinct tells me that there was war in his heart; yes, the words of his mouth were softer than oil, yet I saw swords being drawn. Chei, I saw a campaign of calumny being fashioned against an innocent soul.

Ekemma: Nnanyi, I know you are good at rhetoric, but I will not live to see my daughter writhe in agony under the roof of a rascal. She must make another choice; after all, was it not Dikeoha"s uncle that recounted all these tales? I wonder how someone"s uncle could blackmail him to this extent, if not to protect our interest.

Mkpuruoka: Em! Em!! Woman! Since you have lost your sense of rationality, you can go and decide whatever you deemed fit with your daughter. As for me, my hands are off.

Ekemma: [left to inform Ekechi about the latest development.]

Ekechi: [after hearing from her mother.] Ah! Mama, do you believe this shaggy-dog story? I thought I heard you some months ago extolling and ex-raying the good qualities of Dikeoha. Why the sudden change?

Ekemma: My daughter, you see, all that glitters may not be gold, after all. I was judging him outwardly without knowing his innermost personality. If I may ask, was it not his uncle who knows him better than anyone else, that reveals all his sordid parts to us? As you can reason with me, Upere is a good man; he does not want us to make an unforgivable mistake. Listen, my daughter, you should not restrict yourself to that rascal, think less of him. Go ahead and choose another man of your choice.

Ekechi: Hm, mama, I have heard you. But what does papa say about the unfolding episode?

Ekemma: Em…, your father is devastated by the information; but you should go ahead with your life, hence, Dikeoha is yet to pay for your bride price. He merely came to introduce himself to us. I have to leave you now for my room. Just do exactly what I asked you to do.

Scene II

Dikeoha: [some weeks after Upere"s visit to Mazi Mkpuruoka"s abode, without hindsight, decided to pay an unscheduled visit to his would-be in-laws. At Mazi"s house, he knocked.] Koi! Koi!! Who is here?

Nwanyiorie: [opened the door, with a cold welcome.] Come in now!

Dikeoha: [greeted Mazi and Ekemma.] Nnanyi, I greet you all.

Mkpuruoka & Ekemma: [looking straight and unconcerned.] Hm, you are welcome.

Dikeoha: How about Ekechi?

Ekemma: [being undiplomatic.] Ekechi is indisposed now, and for your information she will be indisposed for a long time to come.

Dikeoha: [becoming anxious] Nnanyi, I wish to know why she is indisposed.

Ekemma: Em, since you demand to know, she is with her incumbent fiancé, Mazi Osueke Abalidiegwu of Rumuazi.

Dikeoha: [striving to curb his curiosity and fury.] Mazi, what is going on here? What am I hearing? Why did you give out my heartthrob to another man?

Mkpuruoka: Hm, Dikeoha, I must tell you, it is hard to chew. You see! Your uncle, Upere came here and told us that you are a rascal and an orphan, who can not take good care of our daughter. He also said that there is an incurable death spell on your family. Finally, he admonished us not to give our daughter"s hand to you in marriage. He went further to enumerate on the would-be consequences, if we act against his advice. Subsequently, we acted in order to protect our daughter.

Dikeoha: [exhibiting wisdom] Mazi, it is not my responsibility to debunk whatever my uncle, Upere had told you, but wait for me tomorrow. I will come with your informant. I have to leave now. Thank you very much. Goodbye.

Mkpuruoka:[as Dikeoha was leaving, began to see his innocence of the allegations.] Ekemma! Ekemma!! Please, make sure that your daughter is here before tomorrow morning. My conscience is pricking me that we have treated Dikeoha unjustly.

Ekemma: Nnanyi, I have heard you, she will be back this evening.

Scene 12

Dikeoha: [at home, unctuously went to Upere and wooed him to accompany him to Mazi"s abode the next day, and he (Upere) sheepishly agreed.] Nnanyi Upere, please, I brought these kola nuts and schnapps to seek your indulgence to accompany me to Mazi Mkpuruoka"s home tomorrow morning.

Upere:[a perpetual glutton.] Thank you my son for the presents. You have exhibited maturity and wisdom. I will definitely follow you to Rumuodara tomorrow.You have very good in-laws. I feel like going there every day.

Dikeoha: Nnanyi, thanks for your concern and encouragement. May your days be elongated.

Upere: iséë oh. Ha! Ha!! Ha!!! Yes, my son, you have spoken well.

Dikeoha:[begged to leave.] Nnanyi, we shall see tomorrow morning for our journey. Good bye.

NEXT DAY

Upere: [the next day, as he was preparing his palm wine for sale, Dikeoha arrived and greeted him.] Yaa, my son, Dikeoha, you are welcome. Please, you should go and come back in the next one hour, before then, I would have finished what I"m doing right now, and also taken my bath and prepared properly for the journey.

Dikeoha: [knowing quite well that, Upere was foot dragging, restrategised.] Nnanyi, don"t bother yourself about me. I will wait here, until you finish whatever you have to do. You see, I have hitherto apprised my neighbours that I was going out on a journey.

Upere: [albeit, disappointed by Dikeoha"s decision to wait, put up make-believe.] Ah! Ah!! You are free to wait; after all, my house is your house. I shall be ready soon.

Dikeoha: [satirically.] Nnanyi Upere, you are right. Perhaps, your house is not only my house but my home.

Upere: [calling one of his little children to take the palm wine to the market for sale] Ebubedike! Ebubedike!!

Ebubedike: Nnanyi, here I"m.

Upere: Now, take this palm wine to the market for sale.

Ebubedike: Okay, nnanyi, I will set out in a jiffy,

Upere: [hastened up.] Dikeoha my son, let's embark on our journey, before the sun sets.

Dikeoha: [on their way.] Nnanyi, our people do say that, he who stood up, knows where he is going.

Upere: You got it right, my son.

Dikeoha: Eureka! I"m happy to have Mazi Mkpuruoka as my in-law. He always accords me and my companions, warm welcome in his abode. Ugh! I know, today"s visit would not be different, especially with your presence, Nnanyi.

Upere: [ironically.] My son! You know that you are a brilliant handsome man, and as such every good household would cherish having you as an in-law. You are wealthy in terms of landed properties. You have the capability of taking goodcare of over a hundred wives. And above all, you are not a scalawag. Your ancestors lived very long. Concisely, you have all the qualities of a good son-in-law.

Dikeoha: Thank you, Nnanyi for the compliments. You always give me hope and confidence, which is the reason why I take you as my father, since the demise of my parents.

Upere: [while smiling grovelingly.] Dikeoha, you can always, even in a fantasy world bank on my inflexible support.

Scene 13

Dikeoha & Upere: [got to their destination; simultaneously enthused.] *Onye no ebe a* (who is here?); *anyi na ekele o…* (we are greeting o…).

Mkpuruoka: Ah! *Obu onye, batawa* (Ah! Who is that, come in).

The Visitors: [entered.] Mazi, *anyi ekele gi, ñno* (Mazi, we greet you, welldone).

Mkpuruoka: *iyaa, ñnonu, unu abiala* (yes, welldone, have you come?). *Ndi obiam wéré nnu óche* (My visitors, have your seats). Hmmn, my people, this is kola nut and some wine, as custom may demand.

The visitors: [after the soft entertainment] Mazi, you have done well, thank you for the hospitality.

Dikeoha: [cleared his throat.] Mazi, em, em, I wooed my uncle to this place to confirm, if actually he made those derogatory comments against me. Please, could you reiterate what you said, he (my uncle) told you about me.

Upere: [became restless. He couldn"t believe his ears] Hei, what is happening here? Am I safe?

Mkkpuruoka: Upere, nothing new is happening, you are safe. I"m a man of principle and justice. It is in my character to remove lice from the cow"s skin and show her the lice so removed.

Upere: Mazi, we know that you are a man of his words, but why this idiomatic expression? Hmm, if we continue unwrapping the wrapper of an old woman, we may uncover faeces o.

Mkpuruoka: Em, this is not the time for idioms and counter idioms. Upere, you came here some market days ago, and told me that your nephew, Dikeoha, is a rascal and an orphan who cannot take good care of my daughter. Above all, you said that there is an incurable death spell on his immediate family.

Dikeoha: [cut in] Nnanyi Upere, did you utter such comments against me?

Upere: Please my son, forgive me, it was the handiwork of *Ekwensu* (the devil), chei, I"m finished o.

Mkpuruoka: Upere! So you lied against your nephew? What an evil world are we living in? How can a man drink his own urine? Dikeoha, my son, please forgive your uncle. Ekechi is back, if you still need her, she is all for you, albeit, there is a little issue to be sorted out.

Dikeoha: [being curious] Mazi, what sort of issue are you talking about?

Mkpuruoka: Hm! I will disclose it to you at the right time. Perhaps, when you pay another visit here.

Dikeoha: Mazi, I will come over, the next *eké* market day.

Upere & Dikeoha: Mazi, we have to leave now, for we have a very long distance to cover on foot.

Mkpuruoka: Dikeoha, please, take things easy with your uncle. As you can see, he has realized his mistakes and asked for forgiveness. As it is said, to err is human and to forgive is divine. I wish you journey mercies.

Dikeoha: [on their way home, lambasted and thrashed Upere.] Upere! So you formulated all these lies against me? Yes, I knew it; you don‟t want me to have my own children, who will in turn inherit my properties. You want me to die as a bachelor, so that your descendants will take over my lands. You are a wicked uncle. I will thrash you with this cane right now, without respecting your foolish old age. Hmm, if not for what my in-law said, I would have maimed or even eliminated you right here.

Upere: [while reeling in pain.] Please forgive me. I said, I‟m rueful. I did not realize that it would come to this extent. Please, don‟t tell anyone at home of what transpired today. I pledged my sincere support to all your endeavours.

Dikeoha: [remorsefully.] Nnanyi, please, I‟m extremely sorry for thrashing you, it‟s because I was emotionally overwhelmed. I have forgiven you.

Upere: Thank you my son, I deserved whatever punishment I might have received from you; such is the price for greed.

Dikeoha: [at home.] Nnanyi, thank you for the companionship, I have restored my trust in you; feel free to associate with me. Goodbye.

Upere: Thanks a lot my son, *Chiokike* will see you through. Goodbye.

Scene 14

Dikeoha: [the next *ekë* market day at Mazi"s abode.] Em! Mazi, you have presented kola nut, thank you very much. Now, what is the issue to be sorted out?

Mkpuruoka:[cleared his throat.] Em, it is hard to chew. Well, as you can see, pregnancy is not what one can conveniently hide from public glare.

Dikeoha: Mazi, what has idiom got to do with a simple question? Who is pregnant? What brought about pregnancy in our discussion?

Mkpuruoka: Youngman, I can see your curiosity, just calm down. Don"t be in a hurry to lick your fingers because you are not going to hang them on the roof.

Dikeoha: Mazi, I have heard you. Your concern is noted. But what is the issue at stake?

Mkpuruoka: [calling his wife] Ekemma! Ekemma!! Please come over here.

Ekemma: Nnanyi, here I"m.

Mkpuruoka: Please, sit down. I have something very touchy to tell Dikeoha about Ekechi, our daughter.

Dikeoha: [still curious.] Mazi, I hope Ekechi is hale and hearty?

Mkpuruoka: Ekechi is well, she even inquired of you some days ago.

Dikeoha: Mazi, you are keeping me in suspense. What really is the issue? As you are aware, no matter how hot the sun is, it cannot ignite a roof. The ear can only tingle after hearing certain events but cannot bleed. Just open the ominous bag for me.

Mkpuruoka: [summoned courage at this juncture, looking at Dikeoha"s mien.] To let the cat out of the bag is to say that Ekechi is a month old pregnant.

Dikeoha: What? How come? For who? Oh… God, why should this happen to me?

Ekemma: It was as a result of the false information divulged to us by your uncle that made us decide that Ekechi should be allowed to have another man in her life. It was during this period that Mazi Osueke Abalidiegwu of Rumuazi came into her life. The result of that relationship is the pregnancy we are talking about here.

Mkpuruoka: Dikeoha, my son, I know it will be hard to chew, that is why I found it clumsy to tell you. It really embittered my soul. But now that you are aware, the ball is in your court, either you take her with the pregnancy as your wife or you forget her for Mazi Osueke who is yet to pay her bride price. Hm, I see you as a worthy youngman with vision, and also having been our family doctor for ages, that is why I deemed it fit to give my daughter to you in spite of the present circumstances. It may not be a palatable pill to chew, but it's worth the stress.

Ekemma: I hope you are aware that our daughter really loves you? If not for the deceitful story from your uncle, things wouldn"t have gone this way. Please take heart.

Dikeoha: [furiously reeling in thought, shaking his head, feet and gnashing his teeth; shudders and sighs.] Mazi! Ekemma! I have heard you all. I will be back tomorrow. Tell Ekechi that, I greet her. When I come, I will tell you my decision on the issue.

Scene 15

Dikeoha: [went to inform Upere at home on what transpired between him and Mazi at Rumuodara.] Nnanyi, Mazi told me that, Ekechi is pregnant for Mazi Osueke of
Rumuazi. I"m now in a fix, what should I do?

Upere: [being rueful.] My son, I"m really sorry for my actions. I"m the cause of the whole saga. I feel like committing suicide. Chei, *aru eme!!!* I hope Dikeoha"s ancestors will forgive me?

Dikeoha: Nnanyi, this is not the time to pass the buck. What should we do now? Should I ditch the marriage arrangement?

Upere: Hm, you can still proceed with the marriage rites.

Dikeoha: [curiously.] Eh! Nnanyi, what about the pregnancy and the child to come?

Upere: [cleared his throat.] My son, our ancestors told us that children are soothed to the heart; yes, they are issues of the heart, where they belong; and as such the heart does not reject children. Children are gift from Chiokike. Besides it is Chiokike, who directs the affairs men.

Dikeoha: Nnanyi, are you saying that, *Nwadinobi* (child is in the heart) and the heart does not reject a child? So *Chiokike's* gift should not be rejected?

Upere: You are right my son. We are going to marry Ekechi. However, the marriage rites will be carried out after she might have delivered the baby.

Dikeoha: Nnanyi, why should the marital rites tarry till after procreation?

Upere: Hmmn, it is a taboo in Igboland to carry out such rites on a pregnant woman (*Igbo anaghi eme ihe nwanyi mgbe odi ime*).

Dikeoha: Nnanyi, may I once again plead for your indulgence to accompany me to Rumuodara tomorrow?

Upere: My son, as long as you have forgiven me for my satanic role in this quagmire, I will follow you anywhere. I pray your parents will pardon me wherever they are, for they beckoned on me to look after you.

Dikeoha: Nnanyi, it is okay, there is no need to cry over spilled oil or broached egg. Em, my parents had forgiven you, hence I have done so. Once again, I wish to express my gratitude to you for accepting to accompany me to Rumuodara tomorrow. Goodnight, Nnanyi; but remember that, we shall leave here very early in the morning to avoid sunset.

Upere: I"m aware of the suntan these days. Goodbye, son.

Scene 16
The Next Day

Upere & Dikeoha: [on their way to Rumuodara, overtook an avalanche of youngsters hurrying to the stream to fetch water, who greeted them and wondered where they were rushing to at that wee hour of the day.]

Youngsters: *Nnanyi, otutu oma* (our elders, good morning).

Upere & Dikeoha: *iyaa umuoma, unu asaalachi* (yes, beautiful children, have you seen a new day?). How are you all?

Youngsters: We are fine. Nnanyi, em, you must be going somewhere very, very important at this early hours?

Upere: You are right my children. A hen does not mesmerize in the rain for the fun of it.

Youngsters: Hm, go well Nnanyi, *Chiokike* and our ancestors will see you through.

Upere & Dikeoha: *iséé o…!* (Amen o…!)

Upere: Dikeoha, you see, we have
well-cultured and industrious youngsters in our community.

Dikeoha: Hm, but Nnanyi, I still wonder why we are retrogressing.

Upere: Ugh! It"s because of the activities of some diabolic men in our midst, who do not cherish seeing others progress. Oh! I really blame myself for treating you the way I did.

Dikeoha: Ah! Nnanyi, forget about that, it"s all now history.

Upere: Hm, my son, history is our life and should not be neglected, because it does repeat itself. However, I got your message of genuine forgiveness.

Dikeoha & Upere: [at Mazi"s residence, after the usual entreaties.] Mazi, you have given us our traditional kola nut and palm wine, thank you very much. Mm! It is now time to talk.

Upere: Mazi, *ñno, imeala* (Mazi, you have done well), em, my nephew told me everything about Ekechi"s condition right now. To be concise, we will come for the marital rites after delivery, as our tradition would demand; in the interim, we„ll come to take Ekechi home in the next two *afor* market days.

Dikeoha: Mazi, please, where is my love, Ekechi?

Ekemma: [cut in.] She is with her chum in the next building.

Dikeoha: Please, extend my felicitation to her.

Upere: Mazi, as you know, we came early here in order to go back in time to attend to other issues at home. On this matrix, we plead to leave. Please, wait for us as discussed. Cheerio.

Mkpuruoka: *Ijeoma, ka chi anyi dube unu* (safe journey, may our God lead you).

Scene 17

On the appointed day, Dikeoha, Upere, Nsiko and three other women went to Rumuodara and brought Ekechi to Rumuoma. She lived with Dikeoha until she delivered a replica of Osueke, a notorious criminal with diabolical powers, who could only be compared to modern-day Lawrence Anini, the terror. After the delivery of the child, Dikeoha went to Rumuodara with his Umunna (kinsmen) and Umundomi (womenfolk) for the marital rites. The rites were carried out in a grandiose fashion.

Umunna: [after the marriage ceremony.] Dikeoha, please tell us the position of this ominous child in our midst. We know the profile of his biological father who is a monstrous criminal. As you know, a snake will always give birth to a long creature.

Dikeoha: Umunna, with all due respect, as I said earlier, the child is to be received and treated as my child, hence the heart does not reject children. Children are soothing to the heart and as such, they are precious gifts from *Chiokike* that ought not to be rejected. I hereby name this child, *Nwadinobi*. Indeed, the oddities of child existence belong to the heart.

Umunna: Dikeoha, this decision of yours is hard to chew, we wish to apprise you that this child will be the harbinger of extreme greed, thievery and diabolical culture in our neighbourhood. Our ancestors used to say that the antelope and her offspring are perpetually adorned in the same cloth. Em! Em!! Do not say, we did not warn you.

Dikeoha: Umunna, I thank you for your concern and also, I appreciate your fears. However, let *Chiokike* take control of our destiny.

Umunna: [while leaving Dikeoha.] The stubborn fly that does not take advice, is destined to follow the corpse to the grave.

Ekechi: [later in the marriage gave birth to two other boys and two girls (from Dikeoha"s gene). These children took after their father"s trait. They followed the path of peace and justice. But the black sheep (Nwadinobi) never allowed them and their parents to enjoy peace, as they were growing, even in adulthood.]

PHASE TWO

The Imp

Nwadinobi:

As the children were growing, having assumed the position of the first son, he became a thorn in the tongue of other children. He started displaying the traits of his biological father at a tender age. He dealt ruthlessly with his parents. He stole their shekels, trinkets, sold their personal effects, harvested their crops such as palm fruits, pears, yam, maize, oil bean (ugba), coco yam, cassava etc and sold the same. He did not spare other people"s goats, dogs, fowls and crops. He was a kleptomaniac. As the first „son", Dikeoha married Nmabaraego for him, hoping that that would curb his rascality, but the gene that produced him was so strong that only his demise can make a change. The father established palm oil mill firms for him. He took Ugwumba, the fourth child, as one of his workers. He promised to train him on a trade and opened a workshop for him. However, after enslaving him (Ugwumba) for many years, he threw him away.

Act Two

Scene 1

Dikeoha: [at home, complaining bitterly about stolen shekels and other personal effects, calling on his wife.] Ekechi! Ekechi!!

Ekechi: Nnanyi, here I'm.

Dikeoha: Ekechi, I have been observing recently that each time I put money in the coffer, right in our room, either the amount is reduced or it disappears miraculously. Just about two hours ago, I put a substantial sum of money in the coffer, only to come back to see nothing.

Ekechi: Humm, chei! Nnanyi, this is terrible. You see, I have suffered the same fate in the recent past. The most painful and mind-boggling thing is the loss of most of my precious jewelry and bottom drawer.

Dikeoha: Tufiakwa! *Ihe a bu aru* (this is evil). What is really going on here? Who is doing these things? Hm, can it be these children? But they are still very immature for such acts.

Ekechi: [cut in.] Nnanyi, I had interrogated the children in the past, but none of them accepted culpability. Hmm, this is ominous, Nnanyi, we have to act fast.

Dikeoha: Listen, henceforth, vigilante should be our watchword. We are going to expose some shekels and pretend as if we are going to the farm while monitoring the house from a hidden corner. I"m optimistic that such booby traps will enable us to track down the culprit(s).

Ekechi: Nnanyi, I think this is a good idea. Only God knows who has been doing these to us.

Scene 2

Dikeoha: [the next day, he placed the shekels as planned and called the wife.] Ekechi! Ekechi!!

Ekechi: [answered while rushing in.] Oéé! Nnanyi, here I"m.

Dikeoha: My dear, I have placed some shekels on top of the table in our room, well-exposed. Please, go and inform the children that we are going to the farm, and that they should take care of the house.

Ekechi: [left and came back after a few minutes.] Nnanyi, I have told them. Let"s desert before anyone starts monitoring our movements.

Dikeoha: [as they were leaving.] You are right my dear, someone may start monitoring us. Yes, a man who is besieged by enemies, does sleep with one eye wide open.

Nwadinobi: [thirty minutes later, tiptoed quietly into his parents" room, so as not to attract the attention of his siblings.] Che! Eeh! So the spider"s web has caught them once again; useless parents, they have been concealing their shekels for some time now. Ugh! At least this shekel will sustain my jollification(s) for some days.

Dikeoha & Ekechi: [suddenly came in as Nwadinobi was rushing to the entrance door with the loot.] Kai! What are you doing in our room? What is in your hand? Hmm! So you are the criminal and the esoteric magic-finger in this house.

Nwadinobi: [rushed out of the room as his parents were reeling in thought.] Hei! Let me tell you people, this is just an iceberg of what is to come. Why are you ranting? Is it because I took what rightfully belongs to me? Am I not the first son? Let me apprise you, next time, I will not tolerate this insult from you o…

Dikeoha: [thoughtfully, not to hurt Ekechi.] Chei, hmm, umunna were right o; a viper cannot forgo its fangs. Chei, chei, tongues will begin to wag. What a shame? How long am I going to live with this?

Ekechi: [observed that Dikeoha was in deep thought.] Nnanyi, you are not talking. I know that this piggy will embellish us with shame. Hmm, I don"t know what to do. We cannot kill him; I am really troubled. I wonder how long we are going to endure this rascality. I don"t know why *Chiokike* wanted things to go this way (she began to weep).

Dikeoha: [gnashing his teeth while consoling Ekechi.] Ekechi, it"s okay, take it easy, he may change in future. We cannot challenge *Chiokike*. Please, wipe your tears. I don"t want outsiders to think that we are having problems.

Ekechi: [as she sobbed out.] Nnanyi, I know you took a very hard decision to accept the baby as your child, even though he was not your blood, as against the position of your umunna. My lord, I promise to be loyal to you all the days of my life.

Dikeoha: My dear, it"s alright. Please don"t blame yourself or anyone for our present ordeal. This is not the time to apportion blame. Let"s think of how to put our house in order to avoid external interference.

Ekechi: Nnanyi, thanks for your understanding and loving kindness. I pray *Chiokike* will see us through this rough passage. Let me go to the kitchen and prepare a meal for the household. It is getting dark for the day.

Dikeoha: Ekechi, please bring Nwadinobi back, don"t starve him of food. I will deal with him myself.

Ekechi: [while continuing with her cooking in the kitchen.] Nnanyi, I have heard you. Your will is my command.

Dikeoha: [while on his settee, began to sing about life"s journey.] *Ije uwa bu nwayo nwayo, ije uwa bu onye ñnocha ólaba* (life journey is slow and steady, anyone whose time is up leaves).

Ekechi: [as Dikeoha was in the state of wool-gathering, Ekechi came in with his nosh.] Nnanyi! Nnanyi!!

Dikeoha: [while striving to recall his senses.] Ah…! Oh heck! Ekechi, are you here?

Ekechi: Yes, Nnanyi, I brought your food. This is water; please wash your hands, my Lord.

Dikeoha: What about the children? Have you given them their own ration?

Ekechi: Yes, Nnanyi. But Nwadinobi is yet to return.

Dikeoha: Em, em, don"t bother yourself about him, he will soon be back. He is still a youngster, rollicking in exuberance.

Nwadinobi: [tiptoed quietly into the children"s apartment and warned his siblings not to alert their parents.] Hei, none of you should tell papa or mama that I"m around, do you hear me?

The children: Yes…, brother.

Ekechi: [later sneaked into the children"s apartment and saw Nwadinobi.] Hei, Nwadinobi, where have you been all the while? Your father has been looking for you. Now, go and take your food, stubborn rat.

Nwadinobi: [took his meal, thanked his mother and went to bed.] Thank you mama, goodnight.

Scene 3

Dikeoha: [the next morning.] Ekechi! Ekechi!!

Ekechi: Nnanyi, *otutu oma* (my lord, good morning).

Dikeoha: *iyaa nwanyioma, otutu oma kwa* (yes, beautiful woman, good morning too). Where is Nwadinobi?

Ekechi: Nnanyi, he followed his siblings to the stream.

Dikeoha: Hmm, what time did he return?

Ekechi: He came back, rather late, last night.

Dikeoha: Did you give him food to eat?

Ekechi: Yes, Nnanyi.

Dikeoha: Did he exhibit any sign of ruefulness about his actions?

Ekechi: Nnanyi, I did not observe any, hence after the meal, he thanked and bade me goodnight, and besides it was very late in the night.

Dikeoha: Okay, when he is back from the stream, lead him to my presence. I will deal with him myself.

Ekechi: [while leaving the scene.] I have heard you, my lord.

The Children: [came back from the stream.] Mama! Mama!! We are back from the stream, come and help us put down the clay pots on our heads.

Ekechi: [as she was rushing out.] My children, I“m coming o. You are welcome.

The children: [after assisting them to put down the clay pots from their heads, they thanked their mother.] Thank you, mama.

Ekechi: Nwadinobi, your father has been asking for you; come on my son, let“s go and see him.

Nwadinobi: [exhibiting chutzpah, grumbled.] This man should not look for my trouble o. Does it mean he did not get my message yesterday? If he tries anything funny today, I will teach him a strange lesson o.

Dikeoha: [Nwadinobi in his presence as requested.] Nwadinobi! Where did you go yesterday after stealing my money? (He did not allow him to say a word, when he collected a strong cane beside him to trash him).

Nwadinobi: [began to struggle for the cane with his father, who later fell down. As he was rushing out of the scene, enthused.] Ugh! This man wants to go to bed before the fowl o. I have warned him several times to leave me alone. Whoever, that knows him should admonish him o.

Dikeoha: [got up and cleaned his body, pretending as if nothing happened.]

Ekechi: [afterward came in.] Nnanyi, where is Nwadinobi?

Dikeoha: [still in excruciating pain.] Didn"t you see him out there?

Ekechi: Nnanyi, your voice has changed, is anything the matter? Why the croak?

Dikeoha: [stoically.] Hm, there is no problem. All is well.

Ekechi: Nnanyi, I have never seen you in this mood before. Please tell me, what is the matter?

Dikeoha: [deeply in thought.] Eewe! Eewe!! Hmm, it has dawned on me now that this boy is really ominous. Hmmn, see how he pulled me down like a bulldozer. Chei! I have invited a community of lizards with my ants infected firewoods o.

Ekechi: Nnanyi, why are you not talking? Did Nwadinobi provoke you?

Dikeoha: [keeping all to himself.] No, there was nothing like that, my dear. Please stop worrying yourself, all is well.

Ekechi: [still in doubt.] Oh, okay o, since you said that, all is well, let"s take it so. Nnanyi, let me go and bring your breakfast.

Scene 4
Three months later

Day after day, people from within and neighbouring villages do come to lay one complaint or the other, all relating to criminal and antisocial acts against Nwadinobi.

Dikeoha: [just came back from his herbal medicinal itinerary, after a very long distance trekking; as he was about to relax his nerves, he saw Akunobi.] Akunobi my brother, you are welcome; please have your seat. Ehm! Who is there, Kawawa…? Please, bring kola nuts for me.

Akunobi: [looking fretful.] Dikeoha, this is not the time for entreaties. Keep your kola nuts!

Dikeoha: My brother, what is the matter? Why are you panting like a wounded lion? Did somebody sleep with your wife?

Akunobi: Dikeoha, I have known you for a very long time now, as a good man, if not so, I would have pounced on you.

Dikeoha: Akunobi, what is the matter?

Akunobi: The matter is that criminal, you called Nwadinobi. He made away with two of my fowls last *eké* market day and today again, he sneaked into my barn and made away with some of my yam tubers and a cock. Hmm! If I get hold of him, I will strangle him to death o.

Dikeoha: Please, how much do these items cost?

Akunobi: I am not asking you to pay me, but warn that criminal in your house to desist from stealing my belongings. The next time may not be palatable for him. I"m going.

Dikeoha: [in a sober reflective mood, when the wife of Obidike, Nwanyiure burst in with her daughter.] Hmm! I"m finished. Chei!

Nwanyiure: [came in and was torched by Dikeoha"s mood.] Nnanyi, *ñno,* are you okay? You look so sad.

Dikeoha: [wearily.] Nwanyiure, I"m okay, it"s just that I"m feeling groggy, as a result of my long journey. How about Obidike, my friend? I have not seen him for some time now.

Nwanyiure: Nnanyi, Obidike is fine. Hmm, Nnanyi, I actually came to inform you that, that criminal in your house, wanted to rape my daughter a moment ago. Just see how he tore her clothing and beat her up, mercilessly. I"m taking it in a lighter mood, because you are a good man. Nnanyi, you have to do something about this rascal before he destroys your reputation and sends you to an early grave o.

Dikeoha: Nwnayiure, please, don"t go any further with this issue. I thank you for your understanding. I will deal with him when he comes back. I will pay for the garments and any medical bills incurred, but don"t let any other person have knowledge of this reprehensible act.

Nwanyiure: Nnanyi, I have heard you, forget about buying new clothing and offsetting medical bills; just warn that criminal in your house.

Dikeoha: Thank you Nwanyiure. I will do my best to call him to order.

Nwanyiure: Nnanyi, how about Ekechi?

Dikeoha: She is not yet back from the market.

Nwanyiure: Please, greet her for me, when she comes back. Goodbye, Nnanyi.

Dikeoha: Goodbye, Nwanyiure. Please extend my greetings to your husband.

Ekechi: [entered the instant Nwanyiure and her daughter left Dikeoha.] Nnanyi, good evening.

Dikeoha: You are welcome. What actually delayed you in the market today? I"m damn too hungry and tired. You know, the children went out to fetch some firewood.

Ekechi: I"m sorry Nnanyi, I saw my brother"s wife in the market when I was about to leave, one thing led to the other and we went into discussion. You should know that women 's discussions consume time. I"m still sorry for the delay. I will make haste to prepare your delicious meal of *ofe* (soup) *ukazi, okporoko* (ukazi leaf and stock fish) and *nri ji* (pounded yam).

Dikeoha: [he did not reveal to his wife all that he had passed through in the hands of the complainants until after the meal.] Ekechi, you see, Akunobi came here and complained that Nwadinobi stole his yam tubers and fowls. Hmm, as if that was not enough crime, Nwanyiure, Obidike"s wife came in with her daughter, complaining that Nwadinobi wanted to rape her daughter. I saw her torn clothing and the bruises on her body.

Ekechi: Chei! Chei!! Nnanyi, this rascality is getting out of hand o. What does a lad of sixteen years know about women?

Dikeoha: You see, if he is aged twenty, we will get a wife for him, maybe he would be influenced by the culminating responsibilities to change.

Scene 5

Nwadinobi"s rascality continued until his parents married a wife for him and thereafter.

Dikeoha:[was in deep thought, when Anoka came in.] Ah! Ah!! Anoka my brother, long time no see, *i biala ndewo* (have you come, wellcome). How about your household?

Anoka: [fretfully.] Dikeoha, my household is okay. I have no time for entreaties, where is that criminal living with you?

Dikeoha: Which criminal?

Anoka: Where is Nwadinobi? I‟m only respecting you, if not; I would have called the entire umunna and reported you to them.

Dikeoha: What did he do? What is the matter?

Anoka: Nwadinobi and his gangsters went to my farm and harvested my palm fruits, yam tubers, maize and others. They sold them at Rumuekpe market.

Dikeoha: Anoka, my brother, please take it easy. I will replace these items back to you.

Anoka: Dikeoha, you are the cause of your own trouble, had it been you listened to the voice of reasoning from your umunna, you would not have been visited by these problems.

Dikeoha: Anoka, you see, umunna might be right in the sight of human beings but may not be right in the sight of *Chiokike*. You know that, it was love and human sympathy that lured me into taking that all-important decision. If it is a cross let me bear it.

Anoka: Well! Dikeoha, I sympathize with your decision. Meanwhile, warn that bastard not to be near any of my properties again. Hmm, you can forget replacement. After all, we do know that he is not a product of your loin.

Dikeoha: Anoka, in as much as I appreciate your concern and forfeiture of your stolen items, I will not tolerate anyone treating Nwadinobi as a bastard. I‟m his father.

Anoka: Dikeoha, I have gotten your message but don‟t let him come across my way again o. Goodbye.

Scene 6

Three years later

Dikeoha: [in a sober reflective mood, soliloquizing.] Hmm, *Chiokike*, what wrong have I done? Umunna warned me, but because of love for a circumstantial child, I"m being ridiculed each passing day. What should I do now, that this boy is becoming a spell and a *tsetse fly on the scrotum*? Chei, umunna will be mocking me now o. Hmm, would it not be wise to get a wife for him, just to see if he will change? Em! Em!! I think this may serve as the magic wand to these acts of rascality.

Ekechi: [entered.] Nnanyi, what is the matter? You looked so sad. Are you thinking about Nwadinobi?

Dikeoha: Hmm, it"s not actually all about Nwadinobi but I have a good plan for him.

Ekechi: Nnanyi (my lord), what plan do you have for him?

Dikeoha: I have thought it wise to marry a woman for him. Perhaps, the sight of a woman around him will impel on him some sense of responsibilities that might curtail his rascality.

Ekechi: Nnanyi, actually, this is a good strategy but he is just nineteen years old. Is he not too young to marry?

Dikeoha: This is the right time for him to marry and exhaust his energy on his wife, instead of misusing it. Hmm, do you know why I married a little bit late?

Ekechi: I have no idea, Nnanyi.

Dikeoha: [while smiling.] It was all because of the state of affairs where I found myself. You see, being an orphan, I have to fend for myself and lay a foundation for myself unaided. These took some time.

Ekechi: Nnanyi, I can see reasons with you. My support is always there for you. Em! Em!! My lord, let me go and prepare your food.

Dikeoha: Thank you, my adorable wife, for your understanding.

Ekechi: Thank you too, Nnanyi.

Dikeoha: [after having his dinner.] Ekechi, I suggest we put our eyes on the ground to search for a good damsel for our son, Nwadinobi.

Ekechi: Nnanyi, why can"t we go for Nwokafor"s daughter, Adamma?

Dikeoha: Which Nwokafor?

Ekechi: Nwokafor Anokwuru of Rumuinyi, the *dinta* (popular hunter).

Dikeoha: Oh! Chei! Ekechi, you really have an eye for beautiful things. I know Nwadinobi would like her. Em… however, by tomorrow, we should intimate Nwadinobi about her.

Ekechi: Nnanyi, you have said it all. Let"s go to bed, it"s late already.

Dikeoha: That"s right my wife. Good night.

Ekechi: Good night, Nnanyi.

The Next Day

Dikeoha: [in the presence of Ekechi.] Nwadinobi! Nwandinobi!!

Nwadinobi: [hurried in.] Nnanyi, here I"m.

Dikeoha: Nwadinobi, we have seen that you have grown to an adult, you are no more the little child of yesterday; so I and your mother have decided to get you a wife.

Ekechi: My son, you are so lucky that both of us are alive to accomplish this feat for you. You see, your father did not enjoy such privilege. I pray, you will not misuse this opportunity.

Dikeoha: Nwadinobi! Nwadinobi!! Nwadinobi!!! How many times did I call you?

Nwadinobi: Nnanyi, you called me three times.

Dikeoha: Now, you are going to face the challenges of life. Very soon, we shall go and show you, your wife-to-be. She is a very good girl from a popular family.

Nwadinobi: Nnanyi, I have heard you, until then. Let me go and see my friend, Diokpa. We have a wrestling contest today at Mbara Rumuoma.

Dikeoha: Nwadinobi, we know you are a great wrestler, but now is a period of great temptation. You see, whenever a man is about to marry a wife, temptations emanate from all angles, so you have to be extremely careful.

Nwadinobi: Nnanyi, as you know, a lion does not give birth to a weakling. Yes! The sound of dynamites and bayonets cannot stop a soldier from going into the battlefield.

Dikeoha: Nwadinobi, you see, when a dog is about to die, it does not perceive the smell of faeces. Hmm, what the dog saw and started to bark had been seen hitherto by the sheep without any hurly-burly. A word is enough for those who are rational. Rascality has a limit.

Nwadinobi: Nnanyi, are you saying that I"m a rascal?

Ekechi: Hei! You recalcitrant child, don"t attempt to talk to your father like that again or else you will not enter this compound again. What is wrong with you? Look at all the good plans he has for you. You don"t even appreciate his efforts.

Nwadinobi: Hmm! Mama, what do you mean by appreciation? Am I not his son? He is just doing what he ought to do, period. I hope you said that, I have grown into adulthood, why not allow me to live my life the way it pleases me?

Ekechi: Look! The mere fact that we said, you are now an adult, does not mean you are mature enough to take life-touching decisions. You need to be guided.

Dikeoha: Ekechi, allow him to go but I promised, he would come back here with an injured arm.

Nwadinobi: Nnanyi, I will prove you wrong. You know that, I am one of the best wrestlers in this community and beyond, even Anufe „the cat" dreads me. He saw the spirit of invincibility in me. Nnanyi, Mama! I"m on my way; see you in the evening after the contest.

Dikeoha: [in the evening, while relaxing on his cane-chair, suddenly saw three young men running towards his house.] Hei! Who is pursuing you? Why are you panting like wounded lions?

The messengers: Nnanyi, it is hard to chew. We are rushing from Mbara Rumuoma, the venue of the wrestling contest.

Dikeoha: [cut in.] Yes, what happened? Tell me!

The messengers: Nnanyi, your son, Nwadinobi was mercilessly dealt with by Anufe, „the cat". He is still lying down on the turf with a broken arm.

Dikeoha: Hmm, chei, I told this boy to be very careful, he wouldn"t listen. Ekechi! Ekechi!! Come and hear what I"m hearing o.

Ekechi: [as she was rushing in.] Nnanyi, what is happening?

Dikeoha: O ya, let"s go and see your son, these youngsters said that he was beaten ruthlessly by Anufe, „the cat" and that one of his arms is broken.

Ekechi: Nnanyi, you said it, but this boy wouldn"t listen. Let"s go and fetch him, perhaps, this may teach him a hard lesson not to disobey his parents or any other elder for that matter.

Nwadinobi: [while writhing on the ground in agony, saw his parents and remembered their advice.] Nnanyi, are you a prophet? All what you said happened.

Dikeoha: Hmm, only if you will learn from your mistakes. Now that you have a broken arm, Dibia Mgborogwu will visit you this evening. By the time he finishes massaging your arm with his pepperish drug, haply, you may learn your first major lesson in life.

Ekechi: Eweeh! Eweeh!! Hoo! Chei! What trauma is this boy leading us into? Nnanyi, what should we do now? He is writhing on the ground.

Dikeoha: Ekechi, this is not the right time to cry over spilled oil. Let"s look for three able-bodied young men who will take him home.

Ekechi: Nnanyi, where are those vibrant youngsters that brought the message?

Dikeoha: Yes! I have to look for them. Ugwu! Uzo! Okochi! Please, help us take Nwadinobi home, carry him with care. I will pay you your wages.

The messengers: [carried Nwadinobi like a log of wood.] Nnanyi, let"s go.

Dikeoha: [at home.] Thank you very much my children. This is your wages as promised.

The messengers: Thank you Nnanyi, goodbye.

Dikeoha: [in a sober reflective mood, suddenly thundered.] Ekechi! Ekechi!!

Ekechi: [swiftly came in.] Nnanyi, here I"m.

Dikeoha: Please, after cooking, boil some water for Nwadinobi. I will personally massage his battered body, especially his broken arm this evening with hot water and *okwuma* ointment, so that his condition will not deteriorate before the arrival of Dibia Ngborogwu tomorrow morning.

Ekechi: Nnanyi, I will do precisely what you said. But, if I may ask, have you sent for Dibia Ngborogwu?

Dikeoha: Yes, I sent one of those youngsters that brought Nwadinobi back.

Ekechi: Nnanyi, which of them? As you know, these youngsters could be easily carried away by games.

Dikeoha: Hm, you may be right, but I trust Okochi, he comes from a very good home. His father is a strict disciplinarian. I"m quite convinced he will deliver the message. Meanwhile, let"s wait till tomorrow and see whether Dibia Ngborogwu will come or not.

Ekechi: You have spoken well Nnanyi; let me go back to the kitchen.

Dikeoha: [while massaging Nwadinobi"s battered body.] Hei, be steady, this is even less painful, compared to what you will suffer tomorrow in the hands of Dibia Ngborogwu.

Nwadinobi: Nnanyi, Chei…!!! This is painful, don"t touch my arm again ooh…, chei I"m finished.

Dikeoha: Have you learnt anything? I know that after your recovery you will reinvigorate your rascality.

Nwadinobi: Hmm! Hmm!! Nnanyi, I have warned you before not to refer to me as a rascal o. I am only responding to the impulse in me. Whatever you see me doing comes from the inside of me. As you know, an antelope wore the same clothing with her offspring. I cannot change myself.

Dikeoha: [talking to himself, gnashing his teeth and shaking his head in total angst.] Hm! Hm!! Chinekeeh! Chinekeeh!! Chei! At times, it is wise for one to listen to his umunna and forfeit individualism. So this anathema will lead me to my grave. *Chiokike*, please, if possible, remove this cup from my sight.

Ekechi: [came in and met Dikeoha in a thoughtful mood.] Nnanyi, what is the matter? Are you through with the massaging? If you have finished, let"s go inside, it"s late already.

Dikeoha: Eeh, hmn, okay, let"s get in; a hawk will remain a hawk till the end of time.

Ekechi: Nnanyi, why such an idiom? I hope all is well?

Dikeoha: Please, let"s get to bed, so that we can wake up on time to prepare for Dibia Ngborogwu"s visitation tomorrow.

Ekechi: [while aiding Nwadinobi inside the hut.] Look, you have to relax your nerves for easy circulation of blood. Sleep well my son. Good night.

Nwadinobi: Good night, mama.

The Next Day

Dikeoha: [very early in the morning.] Ekechi! Ekechi!!

Ekechi: Here I"m Nnanyi.

Dikeoha: I am going to *afor* Rumuoma market to buy some palm wine, bush-meat and kola nuts for our visitor. You should prepare pounded yam and *ofe egwusi* with stock fish *„okporoko'* for him. As you know, Dibia Ngborogwu is so special to our family. We are in the same vocation, taking care of people"s health matters. He specializes in bone treatment.

Ekechi: Nnanyi, I have heard you, please endeavour to return on time...so that I will be able to prepare the bush meat on time too.

Dikeoha: Yes, my wife. I will make haste to be here in due course. Goodbye.

Ekechi: Go well, Nnanyi, let misfortune not see you. *Ijeoma* (safe journey).

Dibia Ngborogwu: [arrived when Dikeoha had long departed for the market.] *Ké ndi nó na ebeá? Onye na nke ya! Onye na nke ya!!. Óbu Dibia Ngborogwu na ekélé* (who are those here? Everyone on his own! Everyone on his own!! It is Dibia Ngborogwu, who is greeting).

Ekechi: [came out.] *Ewuoh! Nnanyi, óbu gi* (Oh! My lord, is it you?) You are welcome. Please have your seat.

Dibia Ngborogwu: Yes, good woman, it is me. Where is your husband? I got his message through *Ókòchi* (the dry season).

Ekechi: Em, he left for the market very early in the morning, he may be on his way back home by now.

Dibia Ngborogwu: Hmn, okay, where is the boy with the broken arm?

Ekechi: He is still lying down on his cane bed.

Dibia Ngborogwu: [went to see Nwadinobi.] My son, how are you feeling? Hmm! This bruise is a complicated one o.

Nwadinobi: Nnanyi, I"m still in pain. I hope after administering drugs on my broken arm, I will be well.

Dibia Ngborogwu: You are right my son, you will be well, only if you can stand the flavor of my drugs. My drugs are not meant for cowards and weaklings; only the courageous and bravery dares my drugs.

Nwadinobi: Nnanyi, as you already know, a lion does not beget a goat. The snake is never perturbed by nightfall, for she is the queen of darkness.

Dibia Ngborogwu: My son, I can see your courage. Let"s get to the bridge first. It is only in the wrestling arena that one can identify amongst the contending tortoise(s), the one that is male.

Dikeoha: [came back from the market.] Ekechi! Ekechi!! Come and carry these items in.

Ekechi: [came out.] Nnanyi, you are welcome. Our visitor is already here o.

Dikeoha: Aha! You see, I told you that *Ókòchi* (the dry weather or season) will deliver my message. Where is he?

Ekechi: He is with Nwadinobi.

Dikeoha: Please, make haste to prepare the food and this meat in time. Let me see him.

Dibia Ngborogwu: [as Dikeoha entered Nwadinobi"s hut.] Ah! Dikeoha are you back? I was told that you went to the market very early.

Dikeoha: Dibia Ngborogwu, you are welcome. I went to the market to get some fresh palm wine.

Dibia Ngborogwu: Did you get any? I learnt that palm wine is scarce and expensive these days. Things have changed o. Our youngsters no longer tap *ñkwuelù* (palm wine tapped from a standing palm tree), instead they go for raffia palm „*ngwo*‟, which is naturally a dwarfing tree. Raffia palm wine is a drink for women.

Dikeoha: Actually, I got one big jar, not without stress and high cost. All the same, I am happy that I came home with some palm wine for my noble friend and occupational colleague.

Dibia Ngborogwu: Dikeoha, you see, I have already planned to go to Ugwunchara, when Ókòchi came with your message, but for old time sake, I had to suspend my trip in order to answer your clarion call.

Dikeoha: Thank you my brother. Thank you very much for exhibiting the spirit of *Nwannedinamba (brotherly spirit, help or concern from outside)*. Chiokike will answer all your genuine petitions. You have already seen my son.

Dibia Ngborogwu: *iséé o (Amen)* and yours too. Your son will be well soon.

Dikeoha: iséé*! iséé!! iséé…o(Amen)* . Let‟s go to the *Obu* (a relaxation hut) for kola nuts, as tradition would demand.

Dibia Ngborogwu: You have spoken well, Dikeoha, it is for the good of the community for elders to be around, so that youngsters would not kill lizards for venison. The dove is used to trading on the road, let alone when she got a message that her distant grandmother is dead. The Zebra cannot discard its stripes. Dikeoha, you are your father‟s son. I hope that your first son will take after you?

Dikeoha: Dibia Ngborogwu! Your message is clear. Now that we have arrived at the *Obu*, tradition has to prevail. Em! This is *oji* (kola nut) and *osé óji* (alligator pepper). Please, bless them.

Dibia Ngborogwu: Hmm! Dikeoha, I have seen the kola nut and *osé óji*, had it not been that, you have already mandated me to bless them, I would have said that, let the king"s kola nut remain with him. That"s by the way. Please, remove your cap and let"s pray.

Dikeoha: Thank you for reminding me. My cap is already off my head.

Dibia Ngborogwu: [cleared his throat.] *Chiokike, chiomumu, chi ihu n'anya, chi idi n'otu, chi enweta edozie, Nnanyi bi n'elu igwe, bia gozie óji nkea, ka anyi ta ya tata ngozi na ogologo ndu na ahu isike. iséé…o* (gods of creation, procreation, love, unity, preservation, our heavenly father come and bless this kola nut, so that we may eat same in good health, long life and progress. Amen o.)

Dikeoha: You have prayed very well, even more than some chief priests.

Dibia Ngborogwu: Thanks for the compliments. Em, tell Ekechi, your wife, to boil some water for me. I hope it is time to get on with serious business. I have to cover some villages today and tomorrow before my trip to Ugwunchara.

Dikeoha: [went to Ekechi in the kitchen.] Ekechi, Dibia Ngborogwu said you should boil some water for him. He wants to prepare the drugs for Nwadinobi"s broken arm.

Ekechi: Nnanyi, I have heard you. Meanwhile the food and meat are ready.

Dikeoha: Keep them, until the massaging and treatment is over for the day.

Ekechi: So shall it be, Nnanyi.

Dikeoha: [after a while, back to the „Obu" with Dibia Ngborogwu.] My brother, the hot water will be ready soon. Em, are you not taking the palm wine? I still have some left, to be taken after the meal.

Dibia Ngborogwu: As you already know, I cannot do without palm wine, especially good ones like this. Please, who tapped this one? It tastes like Nwokenkwo Anowi"s palm wine.

Dikeoha: You guessed right. This is his product. His palm wine is unbeatable in this community. *Chiokike* bestowed this precious gift on him.

Ekechi: [came in with the hot water.] Nnanyi, this is the hot water.

Dibia Ngborogwu & Dikeoha: [simultaneously.] Thank you very much, drop it on the floor.

Ekechi: Okay, Nnanyi, I have done so. Let me go back to the kitchen.

Dikeoha: You are at liberty.

Dibia Ngborogwu: [mixed the drugs and went to Nwadinobi"s hut.] O ya, turn your hand this way, not that way. Okay, be steady; don"t shake your body, so that the drugs will not waste on the floor.

Nwadinobi: [as the drugs were being administered.] Nnanyi, take it easy, it is painful.

Dibia Ngborogwu: Ooh! When I told you that, my drugs are not meant for cowards, what did you say?

Nwadinobi: [displaying stoicism.] Okay, Nnanyi, as promised, I will prove to you that I"m not a weakling, I"m made of sterner stuff.

Dibia Ngborogwu: [Nwadinobi gnashed his teeth as his body; especially his broken arm was being massaged.] My son, it will soon be over, just take heart, I can see that you are not a weakling. You will be okay in a couple of days.

Nwadinobi: Thanks, Nnanyi.

Dibia Ngborogwu: Dikeoha, it"s over for today. Em, Nwadinobi, my son, take care. I will see you in two days before my trip to Ugwunchara.

Dikeoha: My brother, you have done well. Let"s move to Obu and have our meal.

Dibia Ngborogwu: [at the *Obu*, chewing some kola nuts and alligator pepper.] Dikeoha, you see, this boy is very strong o. He refused to cry, in spite of the pressure mounted on the broken arm and the pepperish sting of the drugs. Hmm, what such a hardened youngster would be, should be left for the future to divulge.

Dikeoha: [thoughtfully.] So this man is also a fortune teller. He is right. What this imp will do is presently before us. (He suddenly thundered), Ekechi! Ekechi!! Ekechi!!! Please, bring the food here. My friend and I will eat together today. Serve the children, and later serve Nwadinobi, hence the drugs administered on him. Bring the other keg of palm wine too.

Ekechi: [came in with the food and palm wine.] Nnanyi, this is the food and the keg of palm wine.

Dikeoha: You have done well, my wife. Ehn, Dibia Ngborogwu, my brother, food is ready. Let's pray before we eat; you can still bless the food.

Dibia Ngborogwu: [performing libation, took some of the pounded yam soaked with soup and a cup of palm wine, enthused.] *Chiokike*, take this. *Chiomumu*, have yours. *Ala,* our sustenance, this is yours. *Amadioha*, god of revenge, we did not forget you. *Ndinweala*, our ancestors, small and great, guardians of our compound, may it be well with you. All other gods of our fathers we beacon on you to participate in this meal; iséé…o.

Dikeoha: iséé…o (Amen)

Dibia Ngborogwu: [dashed out after the sumptuous meal.] Dikeoha, you have done well, I have to be on my way now. Greet your wife for me. She is a good cook. I will see your son, next tomorrow as promised. Goodbye.

Dikeoha: *Ya gazie, Chukwu nonyere gi, ijeoma*, (let it be well, God be with you, safe journey); *ka odiri ka anyi siri kwuo* (let it be as we said), good bye.

Scene 7

A year later

Nwadinobi: [dashed back from Rumuekpe market.] Papa! Mama!

Dikeoha & Ekechi: [concurrently.] Yes, what is the problem? Why are you panting like a wounded lion?

Nwadinobi: Em, I"m not sure, I will marry Adamma. I don"t like her, meanwhile, I have seen someone else. We discussed today at the market and she agreed to be my wife.

Dikeoha: Hmm! A Zebra cannot discard its stripes. What is the name of the girl and whose daughter is she?

Nwadinobi: Her name is Nmabaraego (beauty that consumes money). She is the daughter of Ebebe Akpaka.

Elechi: From where?

Nwadinobi: Ebebe Akpaka is from Rumumasi

Dikeoha: [muttering to himself.] Hmm, chei, what will be the fate of my family, when I am gone? Chei! Chei!! Hmm…, from one crook to another. Ebebe Akpaka is a notorious criminal. What a shame?

Ekechi: Nnanyi, you are not talking. Do you know this man and his family background?

Dikeoha: [cleared his throat.] It is hard to chew…

Nwadinobi: [cut in.] Whether it is hard or soft to chew, nobody can stop me from marrying Nmabaraego.

Ekechi: Shut up your mouth, your father is still talking.

Dikeoha: [resigning to fate.] Ekechi! Leave him alone. Let his wish be done.

Ekechi: Nnanyi, are you saying…

Dikeoha: [cut in.] Yes, let his wish be carried out. Nwadinobi!

Nwadinobi: Here I‟m, Nnanyi.

Dikeoha: You will take us to the place in the next *afor* market day.

Nwadinobi: You have spoken well, Nnanyi.

Dikeoha: Em, you will first of all, go to her parents with one or two of your friends with a keg of palm wine and kola nuts, there, your heartthrob will introduce you to her parents. This has to be done before our journey there.

Nwadinobi: Nnanyi, I will do precisely what you said.

Dikeoha: Ekechi, please go and prepare dinner, it is late already.

Ekechi: Nnanyi, dinner will soon be ready, because I have already prepared the soup. Let me go and prepare foo foo.

Nwadinobi: [left for his hut.] Nnanyi, let me go to my hut, see you later.

Dikeoha: That"s right, my son.

Scene 8

After the marriage rites had been carried out, Nwadinobi and his wife, Nmabaraego were given a bigger hut, Dikeoha established two oil mill factories for Nwadinobi.

Dikeoha: Nwadinobi, now you are a complete man with your own family to take care of. You see, realizing the enormous responsibility this will impose on you, I decided to hand over to you two oil mill factories. I will take you to their locations tomorrow.

Nwadinbo: Thank you, Nnanyi; I really appreciate your efforts.

Dikeoha: [muttering to himself.] Hmm, a pig will always bog down in a quagmire, no matter the measure of effort put by the owner to keep it neat; (suddenly, thundered) my son, take care of your wife very well.

Nwadinobi: Nnanyi, I will do exactly that. Permit me to go to my hut; my wife is waiting for me.

Next Day

Nwadinobi: [later in the day, after the oil mill factories had been handed over to him.] Ugwumba! Ugwumba!! Ugwumba!!! Come here.

Ugwumba: [came in to answer the call.] Okay, brother, I"m here. What is it?

Nwadinobi: Em! I want you to serve me in my oil mill factories, after two years, I will sponsor you to learn a trade of your choice and thereafter, I will establish a workshop for you.

Ugwumba: [believing that he was talking with a human being with human milk.] Okay brother, I will do as you said.

Nwadinobi: You will be working in the factory at Kumirukiki while your friend and age mate, Uzoma will be working at the other factory.

Later In the Evening

Dikeoha: [later in the evening, calling his second son.] Kawawa! Kawawa!!

Kawawa: [rushed to Obu to answer his father.] Nnanyi, here I"m.

Dikeoha: [cleared his throat.] Now that Nwadinobi is married, I would like you to look for a girl of your choice for marriage.

Kawawa: Nnanyi, you know that, it is our custom for parents to choose life-partners for their sons.

Dikeoha: You are right my son, but you will be searching too, likewise us. If you see, we will assess her background before final approval.

Kawawa: Nnanyi, I have heard you. See you later, father.

Dikeoha: [muttering to himself.] You see! My blood is exactly like me. Kawawa is so humane and respectful. Nobody hears his voice from afar. He is just like Ugwumba, his younger brother. Chei! How would they be able to cope with this bastard, when I‟m gone? Hmm, *Chiokike* will protect them from the fangs of this monster.

Ekechi: [came in.] Nnanyi, I‟m back from the market.

Dikeoha: You are welcome. How was the situation today?

Ekechi: Nnanyi, things are expensive o. I saw your friend Ovuegbe and he extended his warmest greetings to you.

Dikeoha: Chei, Ovuegbe my friend, *Nwannedinamba*. How is he?

Ekechi: He only complained of his eye problem.

Dikeoha: [rhetorically.] Oh, so that his eye problem is still there?

Ekechi: Nnanyi, were you aware of it before now?

Dikeoha: Ekechi, it‟s a long story. He had that problem when he was attacked by some rascals on his way to Ogoja, where he used to trade. I pray, *Chiokike* will restore his sight.

Ekechi: Nnanyi, let me go and prepare dinner.

Dikeoha: Ekechi, I hope it is time for you to allow your daughters to start cooking our food in this house. If they don‟t do it now and learn the art of cookery, is it when they are married, they would start to learn it?

Ekechi: Nnanyi, if you are not aware, my daughters are good cooks. Most of the meals served in this house are prepared by them. I merely supervise them.

Dikeoha: Okay o, let‟s believe you. Em, we shall have some serious dialogue about Kawawa, after dinner.

Ekechi: I have heard you, Nnanyi.

Dikeoha: [after dinner.] Aha! Ekechi, I told Kawawa to start searching for a wife. I‟m also emploring you to join in the search mission.

Ekechi: Nnanyi, it is good you said this now, you see, I have had my eyes for a long time on Urubedi, the daughter of Okereke, the *Ezeji nke mbu* (number 1 King of Yam) of Rumuosochie. She is a very good girl and also comely. Her parents‟ wealth doesn‟t get over her head.

Dikeoha: Ekechi, you are a precious gift from *Chiokike* to me and the children. You always desire the best for us all. You are more than a diamond. I know our son will appreciate her.

Ekechi: Nnanyi, thanks for the commendation but, what I‟m doing is precisely what I am supposed to do. You are all the essence of my existence, without you, life will be meaningless to me.

Dikeoha: Thanks for understanding your role as a mother and wife. Eem! Ekechi you have to intimate your son, Kawawa with our discussion.

Ekechi: Nnanyi, I have heard you. I will do that tomorrow morning. Let‟s get to bed, it‟s late already.

Dikeoha: That‟s true; we have to go to bed now.

Ekechi: Nnanyi, goodnight.

Dikeoha: Goodnight, my wife. Have a nice sleep.

The Next Day

Ekechi: [intimating his son, Kawawa about the would-be bride.] Kawawa! Kawawa!!

Kawawa: [came in to answer the mother in her hut.] Mama, here I"m.

Ekechi: My son, we have gone a great deal to get for you a humble and beautiful bride.

Kawawa: [cut in.] But mama, I have not seen her.

Ekechi: Don"t be curious, son, I promise you will appreciate her when you see her.

Dikeoha: [walked in.] My son, I have heard all your discussions with your mother. I want to assure you that you will not regret having Urubedi, the daughter of Okereke as your wife.

Kawawa: Oh! Papa, is it Urubedi, the daughter of Ezeji *nke mbu* of Rumuosochie, you are talking about?

Dikeoha & Ekechi: [at the same time.] Yes, do you know her?

Kawawa: Hmm, eehm, yes! We met at *Ibó-Uzò* festival some years back and since then we have maintained a platonic relationship.

Dikeoha: My son, would you not like to have her as your bride?

Kawawa: Papa, that girl is a gem. You underestimated her qualities o. You see, I would be the happiest man on earth, if she accepts to marry me.

Dikeoha: My son, be of good courage, just go and acquaint her with your plans for her, your mother and I will take care of the rest. If you are not aware, Ezeji, her father, is my chum. Just do your bit, all will be well.

Kawawa: [being so excited.] Papa, I will do precisely what you said. Indeed, I will go to her place today in the evening. When I"m back, I will give you the feedback. Em, thank you papa, let me go and prepare.

Ekechi: Kawawa, my son, please trade with utmost diligence, deploy all the diplomatic and sophistry instincts in you, while discussing with her. As you know, she is well-cultured and reads meaning to virtually everything.

Kawawa: Mama, how did you get to know much about her?

Ekechi: My son, you should know that I"m a woman. Em, I have had an eye on her for a long time, hoping that one day, she would become my daughter in-law.

Kawawa: [while smiling.] Ah! Mama…you are wonderful o. I thank *Chiokike* for giving me a mother like you. I have to be going right now. See you all later in the evening, goodbye.

Dikeoha & Ekechi: [at a go.] Goodbye son! We wish you Godspeed.

Scene 9

Kawawa: [came back from Urubedi"s place.] Papa, good evening.

Dikeoha: Good evening my son. How did it go?

Ekechi: [strolled in.] Oh, my son, are you back? How did it go?

Kawawa: It wasn"t easy. It was a great battle of arguments and counter-arguments.

Dikeoha: [being curious.] Yes, but in the end, did she accept your proposals?

Kawawa: Well! At the end of the debate, she smiled and said, she will sleep over my proposal.

Ekechi: *Iya... nwam* (Yes..., my son), you have won her.

Kawawa: But mama, she did not tell me that she had accepted.

Ekechi: My son, you cannot see beyond your nose. You see, any damsel that is well-nurtured can"t tell a man categorically that she has accepted his proposal just like that. Her smile at the end of the dialogue depicts her acceptance.

Dikeoha: [interjected.] My son, that"s right. You will appreciate this fact in days to come. Now, my advice is for you to go back at any time convenient to you, to tell her that your parents will be coming to her place soon to see her parents on the matrix of your proposal. After that, recline to your shell and watch her reaction.

Kawawa: Papa, I will see her tomorrow because anything concerning fresh meat ought to be carried out as quickly as possible, hence any delay may lead to the decay of the meat.

Ekechi: My son, you got it right, the earlier the better. Women appreciate persuasion and dedication. If a woman realizes that, the anticipated zeal and steady-fastness are lacking in a relationship, she jettisons the same.

Kawawa: Papa! Mama! I have heard you all, let me go and relax in my hut.

Dikeoha: That‟s right my son, have a nice rest. Em! Ekechi, please tell your daughters to prepare our dinner.

Ekechi: Okay Nnanyi, dinner will be ready in a jiffy.

The Next Day

Kawawa: [intimating his parents on the outcome of his latest dialogue with Urubedi.] Papa! Mama! I must thank you for your gold dust advice and concern. Well, to cut a long story short, she accepted all what I said and promised to intimate her mother about our relationship.

Dikeoha: Meanwhile, I will advise you to visit her parents with one or two of your friends and introduce yourself to them.

Kawawa: Nnanyi, I will do that soon. I beg for your indulgence to leave, so that I will be able to inform my chum and age mate, *Dinta* (the hunter) about my plans and plead with him to accompany me to my finaceé‟s place.

Dikeoha: You have my blessings, son.
Ekechi: May it be well with you, my son. Go in peace.

Three Months Later

Kawawa: [some months after his marriage rites to Urubedi.] Papa! Mama! I shall be going to Lagos to join the army, in three days to come.

Dikeoha: My son, are you sure that you want to become a soldier?

Kawawa: Yes, N nanyi.

Dikeoha: My son, I know you are courageous and physically fit with an intimidating stature. Hm, we shall miss your absence at home. All the same, I wish you success. God will see you through.

Ekechi: My son, I wish you godspeed. Please take good care of your wife, when you get there. God will be with you.

Kawawa: I thank you very much for appreciating my position. I will always communicate with you through telegraph. Excuse me to see my friends in my hut.

Dikeoha: You can leave, my son. Em, Ekechi, have you heard from our son, Ugwumba, since he went back to Kumirukiki, after Kawawa"s traditional marriage ceremony?

Ekechi: Nnanyi, I forgot to inform you that I received a message while in the market from Okembe of Kumirukiki. He said that our son, Ugwumba, is passing through hell in the hands of his brother, Nwadinobi.

Dikeoha: [in a pensive mood.] Hmm, Chei! Chei!! *Chiokike*, please save my son from the fang of this bastard. Did he not promise to train Ugwumba on a trade and open a workshop for him? What is he using his income for? Why is it that he is not progressing? I learnt, he is involved in the act of paying tributes to witch doctors. Chei! Are we safe? It is really true that an antelope does not discard its stripes.

Ekechi: Nnanyi, you have not said anything to what I told you. Are you really okay?

Dikeoha: I"m okay; it's just that I was striving to reflect on what Ugwumba is passing through. Em… Ekechi, there comes a time in a man"s life…when the jewels cease to sparkle…when gold loses its luster…when the throne room becomes a prison and all that is left is a father"s love for his child.

Ekechi: Nnanyi, we have to call Nwadinobi and talk to him.

Dikeoha: If we do that, the situation will worsen. He will think that it was Ugwumba who intimated us about the situation of things over there.

Ekechi: What should we do then? Are we going to sit down here and watch our son suffer untold hardship? We have to do something.

Dikeoha: Well! I can see the concern of a mother for her child. You see, this passage will help to build him up as a man. What he needs most now is perseverance.

Ekechi: Hmm! Nnanyi, is that what you have to say?

Dikeoha: Please, go and get me my palm wine, we will talk about that later.

Scene 10

Dikeoha: [listening to a telegraphic message from Kawawa as being analysed by Uwadiegwu, the village scribe.] Ekechi! Ekechi!! Come and hear what our son is saying in his „wire" to us.

Ekechi: [rushed out from the inner hut to answer Dikeoha.] Nnanyi, here I"m.

Dikeoha: Listen to what Uwadiegwu is saying. He said that our son, Kawawa, sent his greetings to us and that his wife gave birth to a baby boy last month. Our son said that he will come home by next month to see us.

Ekechi: [began to sing while praising God.] *Chineke! Idinma o, Idinma, Idinma o, Idinma, Idinma, Idinma o... Obughi ma nwa onye ga enye m* (twice). Iya! Chiokike has done marvelous things for us.

Nwadinobi: [whose wife also gave birth last month to a baby girl, suddenly came in.] Nnanyi, I greet you. Mama, how are you? I can see that you are all happy. What are you celebrating?

Ekechi: Your brother, Kawawa sent a telegraphic message to us, telling us that his wife gave birth to a bouncing baby boy last month.

Nwadinobi: [in deep thought.] Hmm! So he had a male child before me. That is to say that his children will lord it over my children! Never, over my grave. We shall see.

Ekechi: Nwadinobi! What is the matter? Didn"t you hear what I said?

Nwadinobi: I heard you, I was reflecting on how you will go to far away Lagos for *Omugwo*.

Ekechi: The issue of Omugwo should be waived for now, let"s thank God first for what He has done for us. We have begotten a grandson.

Nwadinobi:[muttering to himself.] Mmh! So you people love and appreciate him more than me? I will deal ruthlessly with you people, afterall; he is not around to protect you from my claws. You are all idiots. As for Ugwumba, I will throw him away.

Dikeoha: Nwadinobi, how about your family and your brother, Ugwumba?

Nwadinobi: [putting up a bold face.] They are fine. Nnanyi, I have to go back before it"s late.

Ekechi: Why are you hurrying back so soon? Why not join us to celebrate the arrival of a grandson in our family?

Nwadinobi: [ignored his mother.] Nṇanyi, goodbye.

Dikeoha: Ekechi, what did you observe in the attitude of Nwadinobi?

Ekechi: He seemed not to be happy with the message from Kawawa and this portends a great danger ahead. Em! Thank God, we did not tell him that Kawawa will come home soon.

Dikeoha: Well! Let"s watchout! Hmm, any child who insists that his mother will not sleep, he also, will not sleep.

Scene 11

Ugwumba: [came back from Kumirukiki, three weeks after Nwadinobi"s visit at home and narrated his ordeal and how Nwadinobi chased him out of the oil mill factory.] Nnanyi, you know that, I"m not garrulous.

Dikeoha: Yes, my son. I have known you right from infancy, you seldom lie; taciturnity is your nature.

Ugwumba: Nnanyi, I"m not going to talk about my ordeal with my brother, Nwadinobi, but I just want to apprise you that he sent me packing from Kumirukiki. Now, I have come back empty handed, after years of slave labour.

Dikeoha: My son, I"m not surprised to hear this from you. We, here, had been informed about your ordeal by different personalities from Kumirukiki. I will tell you right now, not to be perturbed. When your brother, Kawawa comes back this week, I will implore him to take you to Lagos.

Ugwumba: Thank you papa, for your inspiring fatherhood.

Ekechi: [came in.] Ah! Ah!! My son, when did you come? How are you? You looked so malnourished.

Dikeoha: [cut in.] Ekechi, please be less curious, I will intimate you later on what he had passed through in the hands of Nwadinobi. Allow him to go in and have some rest. I hope there is food in the house for him to eat?

Ugwumba: Mama, I will see you later; let me go and have some rest as father had said.

Ekechi: My son, whatever it is, keep your cool. I will soon come to serve you some food.

Dikeoha: Ekechi, please go in and see your son, I want to go and see my friend Nwogu, the *Diochie* (palm wine tapper) of Rumuagu.

Ekechi: Nnanyi, I have heard you. I wish you a safe journey to Rumuagu.

A week later

Kawawa: [came back from Lagos.] Papa! Mama! I‟m back oh.

Ekechi: [came out of the hut.] Eeh! Eeh!! Eeh!!! Chei! *Chiokike*, you are great and wonderful. Chei, my son, you are welcome. How about your wife and our grandson?

Kawawa: Mama, all is well. My wife extended her felicitation to you all. She also sent some prezzies to you.

Ekechi: Uuuh! Mmm! So my daughter in-law sent all these items to me? Oh! God will bless her and see her through in all her genuine endeavours. My son, who is bathing the new baby, since I‟m not doing that as tradition would demand. As you know, Lagos is a very far place from home.

Kawawa: Mama, I‟m here to take you to Lagos for pseudo-omugwo.

Ekechi: [visualizing Lagos as a wonder land.] But my son, Lagos is very far and we heard that vehicles do fly in the air. We also learnt that there are floods of criminals who maim and kill people in Lagos. My son, do you really think I can fit into Lagos life?

Kawawa: Mama! Ah! I can see your curiosity, you see, Lagos is a very big city, there is hardly anything that one cannot find there. I will take care of you, so you have nothing to worry about. Please start to prepare right away; get all the necessary things you may need over there ready. We shall be travelling to Lagos in two day‟s time.

Dikeoha: [came in, as Kawawa was about to end his discussion with his mother.] Ah! Ah!! My son, when did you come? How about my daughter in-law and my grandson?

Kawawa: My wife sent her warm greetings to you. My son is fine and kicking.
Ekechi: My son let me go and prepare some food for you. Excuse me, Nnanyi.

Dikeoha: My son, we got your telegraphic message and prezzie. Thank you very much.

Kawawa: Papa! You don‟t need to thank me for anything. I‟m just performing my duties. You see! You brought me up, right from childhood to adulthood; so you are reaping the fruits of your labour. He who works deserves a wage. I‟m lucky to have you and mama as parents.

Dikeoha: Thank you, my son, for appreciating our little contributions. Your own children will accord you the same respect.

Kawawa: Papa, what about Nwadinobi? I learnt his wife gave birth to a baby girl. What about my younger brother, Ugwumba?

Dikeoha: Hmm! Nwadinobi is a thorn in our tongue. You have to be diplomatic when relating with him. He threw Ugwumba away after enslaving him for a long period.

Kawawa: But, where is Ugwumba now? I will go to Kumirukiki tomorrow to see Nwadinobi.

Dikeoha: Ugwumba went out with his chum and age mate, Uzoma, who was also fired without compensation by Nwadinobi. Em! Em!! I wouldn"t advise you not to go to Kumirukiki, but tread with care, for Nwadinobi had an angry look. He is a green-eyed monster and as such, very dangerous. Make sure you don"t drink or eat in his house. You see, I"m not trying to bring division between you, but I can"t afford to see you and Ugwumba destroyed by someone endowed with the spirit of greed. A word is more than enough for the rational soul.

Kawawa: Nnanyi, it is always said that the words of elders are the words of wisdom. It is better to listen and appreciate the scolding of a wise man than to listen to the songs of a fool. A dutiful hen will always protect the chicks from the claws of the hawk.

Dikeoha: You have spoken well, my son. A tortoise does not visit the market without looking sideways. A dove begets a dove. You are the true son of your father.

Ekechi: [came in.] Nnanyi, I beg to take Kawawa temporarily away from you. His food is ready. But, meanwhile he had to go and take his bath.

Dikeoha: My son, your mother is right, go and have your bath and food, we shall discuss other issues later.

Ugwumba: [walked in, as Kawawa was about to leave.] Ah! Brother! When did you come back? How about your wife and kid?

Kawawa: They were okay, when I left them. Mm! Papa told me about your predicament with Nwadinobi. We shall dialogue later on the next line of action.

Ugwumba: Thank you, brother; I appreciate your brotherly concern.

Scene 12

Next Day

Kawawa:[at Kumirukiki.] Brother! How about your business and family?

Nwadinobi: As you can see, things are going on very well. My wife went to collect her ostentatious clothes from her tailor, at the adjacent building. Em! When did you return from Lagos?

Kawawa: I came back yesterday.

Nwadinobi: When are you going back?

Kawawa: [meditating.] Hmm! Why all these quizzes? He did not even ask about my wife and kid, let alone my job. I will not open up to him. I can now smell a rat. Chei! Papa was right o.

Nwadinobi: Kawawa! You have not answered my question. When are you going back to Lagos?

Kawawa: Brother, as you can see, I just came in yesterday. So I have some time to spend at home.

Nwadinobi: Hmm! That would be nice.

Nmabaraego: [walked in and gave Kawawa a lukewarm felicitation.] You are welcome.

Kawawa: [smelling a rat.] Yah! Our wife, how about your baby?

Nmabaraego: She is okay. Em! Em!! Excuse me, I have some business to take care of in the kitchen.

Nwadinobi: [as Nmabaraego was approaching the kitchen, called her aside and whispered to her to add some poison into the food, but voices out a different thing.] Nma! Please prepare a delicious meal for my brother; he must be very hungry, having come a long distance.

Kawawa: Brother! Ah! Don"t bother yourself as I told you during the presentation of kola nuts, I took a purgative drug and as such, I can"t take anything for now.

Nwdinobi: Kawawa! What is fishing? I gave you kola nut, you rejected it, and now you said you are not going to eat my food, on the flimsy excuse of taking a purgative drug. What did they tell you at home?

Kawawa: Ah! Brother! Why are you talking like this, nobody told me anything o or do you have something to tell me?

Nwadinobi: No, I don"t have anything to tell you really, it is just that, I"m baffled at the rejection of my food by my own brother.

Kawawa: Brother! Try to understand; since I joined the army, my orientation about health issues have changed. At this juncture, I will advise you not to take any food or water after taking purgatives or emetic.

Nwadinobi: Ewuo! Hmm, so we have gotten an *„ọyibo dokinta'* in our family. Oh…let us wait and see this new trend.

Kawawa: Brother, I have this little token for you.

Nwadinobi: [not being appreciative, pointing at the table.] Mm! keep it on top of that expensive table over there.

Kawawa: Brother! I have to leave now, as you are aware, the journey ahead is very far. Greet your wife for me.

Nwadinobi:[did not escort Kawawa.] Mm! Okay, bye, bye.

Kawawa: [while on his way home, began to soliloquize.] What is the matter with Nwadinobi? Is he really from our father"s loin? Where did he acquire this greedy trait from? Hmm, thank God, papa warned me beforehand. Chei! Ugwumba must have passed through hell under him o. But come hell or high water, he should be stopped from disturbing our parents.

Dikeoha: [at home with Kawawa.] My son, how was your trip to Kumirukiki?

Kawawa: Papa, just as you predicted. I was treated like a total stranger. Hmm! Nnanyi, I know, this may sound ridiculous but at times, I do wonder if actually, we came from the same loin. None of us has anything in common with him and he bears no resemblance to you.

Dikeoha: Kai! My son, there are some questions children do not ask their parents. Hmmn, Nwadinobi is your brother.

Kawawa: Papa, as you have said, I rest my suspicion.

Dikeoha: Ehn, my son, I want to make one request from you and I know, you will not disappoint me.

Kawawa: Nnanyi, just say it, if it is within my powers, I will do it.

Dikeoha: Em! Em!! It"s about your younger brother, Ugwumba.

Kawawa: [cut in.] Yes! What about him? Is he okay?

Dikeoha: My son, please, I want you to take him to Lagos for the meantime.

Kawawa: Ah! Papa, is it what you are begging for? You see, I have already planned to take him to Lagos alongside mama. As tradition would demand, mama has to perform her *pseudo-omugwo* rite, after which my mother in-law will come for the *omugwo* proper. Mm, after a year, I will send Ugwumba back to learn a trade of his choice at home.

Dikeoha: My son, you have spoken well. You are indeed of my loins. The tortoise does not bear a fool for a son. God will crown your endeavours with huge success.

Kawawa: iséé *o(Amen).* Nnanyi, may I remind you that our journey back to Lagos will be tomorrow.

Dikeoha: My son, God will grant you all, journey mercies.

Ekechi & Ugwumba: [came back from the farm.] Nnanyi, we greet you.

Dikeoha: Yaa, you are welcome. How was the farm?

Kawawa:[cut in.] Mama welcome, how did it go today at the farm?

Ekechi: It went well, my son. The yams, coco-yams and cassava are all doing well. Em! Em!! How was your trip to Kumirukiki?

Dikeoha: [cut in.] Kawawa did not find it easy with his brother, Nwadinobi. He was received coldly.

Ekechi: Chei! When will he change? Kawawa, my son, please take it easy with him; that's his nature.

Kawawa: Thank you mama, for your concern. I hope you have put everything in place against our trip to Lagos tomorrow.

Ekechi: Aha! I"m through with my preparations except for one or two infinitesimal touches.

Dikeoha: Ugwumba! Ugwumba!!

Ugwumba:[displaying obeisance.] Nnanyi, here I am.

Dikeoha: You see, your brother has decided to take you to Lagos tomorrow. I wish to admonish you to respect him and his wife; serve them diligently and do not bring reproach to this family. I know you are a fine and humble youngster from my loins. You will always do us proud wherever you find yourself.

Ugwumba: Nnanyi, I thank you for the sagacious advice, I will not disgrace the family in any way. Nnanyi, it is only *udele* (the vulture), who will say that, her pregnancy does not give her any concern, because to her, if the chick is born alive naturally it becomes her baby but if the chick is stillborn, it invariably becomes a meat to be feasted upon. To me, the name of my family is more important than silver and gold.

Dikeoha: My son, you have spoken well. Mbekwu (the tortoise), does not express any fear whenever she sends out any of her offspring as an emissary, *Chiokike* will be with you.

Ugwumba: Thank you, Nnanyi. Thank you too, brother Kawawa, for finding me worthy of joining you in Lagos. I will not disappoint you. May I seek your indulgence to leave now?

Ekechi: Nnanyi, let me go and tell our daughters to prepare dinner. I will be back in a jiffy to give you some life affecting gist.

Kawawa: Nnanyi, permit me to go and see my age mates at *okpoduru-ulo*. I will be back soon, hence my journey tomorrow.

Dikeoha: You are at liberty to leave. Thanks for your sagacity.

Scene 13

Next Day

Dikeoha:[bidding his wife and children farewell.] Chei! My sons, *Chiokike* will protect you and your mother. You will get to Lagos safely. Hmm! Ekechi, so you are leaving me here alone. Okay o, when you come back, I will likewise travel to a far country and abandon you to suffer solitude.

Ekechi: Nnanyi, don"t worry, I will soon be back. After all, it"s just a *pseudo-omugwo*.

Dikeoha:I know that by the time you come back from Lagos, you will be speaking *oyibo* language. Mm! Meanwhile, let me apprise you in anticipation. If you learn your novel language, it shall be for your women forum and not for me.

Ekechi: [while smiling.] Nnanyi, no matter what I learnt or what position I found myself in, I"m still your wife.

Kawawa: Papa, please hold this little shekel for your snuff and kola nuts.

Dikeoha: Chei! My son, you call this money little? This will serve me for a long time to come.

Kawawa: Papa, the motor that will take us to Lagos is around. Mama, Ugwumba, you should pack in the loads in the vehicle.

Ugwumba: [as the car was zooming.] Papa bye, bye.

Ekechi:[rushed to her husband.] Nnanyi, I forgot to tell you this yesterday.

Dikeoha: What is it?

Ekechi: Nnanyi, somebody will soon come to ask for the hand of our daughter in marriage.

Dikeoha: Eeh, do you have any clue as to where the man in question comes from?

Ekechi: Em! Meanwhile the picture is not all that clear but I overheard our daughter mentioning Rumuokwe.

Kawawa: Mama a…, come let"s go, you will soon come back to meet papa. The journey ahead is pretty far.

Dikeoha: Ekechi, please go and meet them, until you come back, remain blessed.

Ekechi: Nnanyi, bye, bye.

Kawawa: [while waving to Dikeoha.] Papa! Bye, bye.

Dikeoha: Goodbye my son. *Chiokike* will see you through.

Ekechi: [while on their way to Lagos.] My son, this motor is different from *Ugbonwaeze*. I am feeling cold; the breeze that is coming in here is too much.

Kawawa: Oh, mama, I forgot to wind up the windscreen. Mama, we shall stop briefly on the way to have some refreshment.

Ekechi: Kai! Kai!My son, so you have forgotten that, it is a taboo in our community for a married man or woman to go to the hotel to eat or drink…

Kawawa: Mama, you are in a different environment and also on a long journey, so tradition does not come into play here. You have to eat, nobody is watching you here.

Ekechi: My son. You have said your own o. I still maintain my stand. If nobody is watching me, our ancestors are watching me.

Kawawa: Em! Ugwumba, please endure; we will soon get to Lagos. I don"t want mama to see us as uncultured children. Let"s just make her happy with her belief.

Ugwumba: Brother, I appreciate your position. I have endured more serious starvation in the past while working for Nwadinobi.

Ekechi: [pointing to storey buildings.] My son, what am I seeing?

Kawawa: Mama, we call them upstairs.

Ekechi: What is it for?

Kawawa: People live in them.

Ekechi: Are you saying that human beings live in them? Mm! Any person that resides therein must be a wizard or witch, hence such can fly.

Kawawa: Ah! Mama, it is not true. You see, *Oyibo* erected these houses and also provided something like an *ubibi* (ladder) called staircases, one can use it to climb from one floor to the other. Mama, don"t worry, when we get to my apartment in Lagos, you will see what I"m talking about.

Ekechi:[as she was in a slumberous mood and yawning.] Hmm…! I have heard you o…

Scene 14

Kawawa: [on arrival in Lagos, tapped the mother.] Mama, get up, we have reached Lagos.

Ekechi: [woke up and yawned.] Oh! My son, is this where you live?

Kawawa: Yes, mama.

Ekechi: Where are your wife and child?

Kawawa: They are in the house. My wife can not open the door until she is sure that I"m the one at the door. Urubedi! Urubedi!! I"m back o!

Urubedi: [she opens the door.] You are welcome, Nnanyi. Mama, you are welcome, Ugwumba you are welcome. I"m happy to see you all. Mama, please give me your luggage and follow me.

Kawawa: [pointing to a room.] Ugwumba, go into that room and change your attire; that will be your room for now.

Ugwumba: Thank you, brother.

Ekechi: [after having her bath and food.] My daughter, where is my grandson?

Urubedi: Mama, he is on the children"s bed.

Ekechi:[she approached the netted cot] Ah! Kai! My son, you people call this thing bed? This is a cage for animals and birds.

Kawawa: Mama, it is not true. You see, this is meant to protect the child from mosquito bites.

Ekechi: Oow! I see… chei! Ignorance is a disease that can only be cured by awareness. Well, now that my grandson is fast asleep, I have to relax my nerves after a long journey.

Urubedi: You are right mama. Mama, I appreciate all the things you brought from the village for us. Thank you very much.

Ekechi: My daughter, you see, I will not stay long here. Your mother will soon come for the *omugwo* proper; hence she is the rightful person to come. I only came to pay homage to my grandson.

Urubedi: Thank you very much mama for your understanding.

Ekechi: Thank you my daughter for giving us a grandson. I will call him Ugombachukwu (the eagle of God"s community). I"m aware that your mother will also give him her own name.

Urubedi: Mama thanks again. You have spoken well. I"m lucky to have you as a mother-in-law. May I seek your indulgence to go and attend to other duties?

Ekechi: Permission granted. My daughter, you are a jewel to your husband and by extension to all of us. *Chiokike* will be with you.

Scene 15

A month later

Dikeoha: [as he was relaxing on his cane chair, saw a car approaching his compound and on a closer view, he saw his wife and son, Kawawa. He thundered.] Hei! Hei!! My son, you have brought your mother back. How about your wife, son and Ugwumba over there? I can see that your mother is well–nourished. Ekechi, you are welcome, my wife. I thought you would not come back again o.

Ekechi & Kawawa: Nnanyi, *nno*, how are you?

Dikeoha: I"m as you left me. *Chiokike* is our shelter. Hmn, your brother, Nwadinobi came here and threatened to bring down hailstone and fireball.

Kawawa: Ehn! What is the matter this time around?

Dikeoha: He accused your mother and me of having more affection for you and Ugwumba than for him. He also frowned that you did not apprise him before you left for Lagos. In short, let"s leave him alone, this is not the right time to deliberate on such an issue. You people should go inside and refresh yourselves after such a long journey. Mm! Before it escapes my memory, who owns this Land Rover?

Kawawa: Nnanyi, it‟s my official car. Nnanyi, I will leave by tomorrow morning with my mother in-law, who will continue from where mama stopped for the *omugwo* proper. I have some grog and schnapps for you. I beg to leave because I need some rest.

Dikeoha: [while sitting alone, mutters to himself.] Ehn! Chei! Look at these children o. They always buy expensive clothes, jewelry, beverages and other good things for their mother, only to come here and present hot drinks and tobacco to me. Does hot drinks and tobacco add anything to our life span? Hmm! Well, I can‟t protest openly because their mother may think that I‟m jealous.

Ekechi: [came to Dikeoha after refreshment.] Nnanyi, where are your daughters, Adaku and Uluaku?

Dikeoha: They went to the market. I hope they should be on their way home by now.

Ekechi: [as Dikeoha was talking, saw her daughters approaching from a distance.] Nnanyi, I have seen them coming. Nnanyi, Lagos is very nice o. I saw *Nwabekeé* (white people) over there.

Dikeoha: [being witty.] I can perceive the scent of Lagos on your body. You are comely plump. Check out the attire, jewelries and beverages packed for you by your son. Em! Are you the one who advised him to buy hot drinks for me, so that I will not be rational enough to see what he bought for you?

Ekechi: Nnanyi, I hope you are joking? Is it not traditional for a son to buy hot drinks and snuff (grounded tobacco) for the father, while returning from a journey?

Dikeoha: [laughing and being pawky.] What sort of tradition is that? Why didn"t the same tradition give room for women to accept schnapps and tobacco while men accept expensive apparels, beverages, jewelries, boxes, food and so forth? My

Ekechi: [while chuckling.] Nnanyi, do you want to change the tradition? Em! If this is to be upturned, automatically, other aspects will also be transformed.

Dikeoha: [beaming with smiles.] What other aspects are you talking about?

Ekechi: Mmm…! Like the women being the lord of the family, and also, mounting on top...during coition.

Dikeoha: [while reeling in laughter.] Chei! Tufiakwa! *Chukwu ekwela ihe ojo*. God forbid evil! It is an abomination.

Ekechi: Oh…Nnanyi, you see! One can not eat his cake and still have it. As you are aware, children are like benevolent spirits. They always recall what we (women) passed through while bearing them in our womb and beyond. They also recognize the roles of their fathers in their existence, which is why they consult them on important issues.

Dikeoha: Ekechi, you may be right, but we are not talking about a son recognizing the roles of his father in his life; we are talking about what children usually buy for their parents. Why the partiality? Why should gender be the determinant factor here?

Ekechi: Nnanyi, you should not bother yourself, after all, both of us will consume the beverages and you will have some of the wrappers for your native attire.

Dikeoha: My wife, you see, my own case is a special one, because *Chiokike* gave me back my missing rib. What about those men who are hen-pecked?

Ekechi: [as the children came in.] My daughters, how are you? I learnt you went to the market.

The children: Yes, mother. When did you come back? What about Ugwumba, brother Kawawa and his household?

Ekechi: I came back this evening and everybody is okay. Kawawa is in his hut, he is relaxing after the long journey.

The children: You are welcome mama, let"s go and see brother Kawawa.

Dikeoha: [saw some women coming to his compound.] Ekechi, you see, some of your womenfolk are coming to greet you. I hope you have some gift items for them, as tradition would demand?

Ekechi: Nnanyi, I will bash them with assorted gifts. My son really made me proud. He anticipated such, and made provisions for the same. Umundomi will be amazed.

Umundomi: [as they arrived in the compound, began to sing and dance in honour of the newborn child.] *Eeeeee...uuuh, o bughi ma nwa, onye ga enyem?* (Repeat thrice) *Egwu otu ukwu abiala, mmai nkwu* (repeat thrice) *Nwa ana amu amu o, Osi na chineke bia o yes!* (Repeat thrice) *O ga m bia lele mmai nkwu* (repeat thrice), Dikeoha *bia lele mmai nkwu* (repeat thrice), *Kawawa bia lele mmai nkwu* (repeat thrice) *Ekechi bia lele mmai nkwu* (repeat thrice), *Urubedi bia lele mmai nkwu* (repeat thrice), *Nwa ana amu amu o, Osi na chineke bia o mmai nkwu!* Uuuuuh.......

Ekechi: [as the women were singing and dancing, rushed out with perfumed powder to welcome them.] *Umunwanyi ibe m, unu abiala eh?* (my fellow women have you come?) *Unu hùrù powder biko* (rub powder please). You have made me proud by rejoicing with me on this day. God will also answer your supplications and reward you abundantly. Please, take your seats.

Umundomi: Ekechi, *imela ezi nwanyi* (Ekechi, you have done well, good woman).

Dikeoha: [came out to greet the women.] *Umundomi, unu abiala? Nno nnu* (women have you come? Well done). *Chukwu gozie unu nile* (God bless you all). *Udo dikwara unu nile* (peace be unto you all) iséé o...

Umundomi: Nnanyi, *udo nke chukwu dikwara gi* (our lord, may the peace of the Lord, also be with you)

Ekechi: [went into the hut and came out with some prize gift items.] Please, my fellow women, I sincerely appreciate your concern about my trip to Lagos and the birth of my grandson. May you please accept these tokens from me. *Chiokike* will increase the fruits of your labour.

Umundomi: [started singing while eulogizing their host with appropriate dance style, after which they thanked her for the gifts.] Ekechi, what you have just given us can not be described as a token. They are well packaged gifts from a large heart. We can't find words to thank you, but just accept our profound appreciation. By this time next year, we will come again for another celebration of a boy from Kawawa. We have to leave now, in order to attend to our husbands and children's needs.

Ekechi: My fellow women, I greet you once more for the honour so far exhibited. Chiokike will answer our entire genuine request. Greet your various households for me. Goodbye.

Umundomi: [as the womenfolk were deserting the scene.] Ekechi, bye, bye o, see you tomorrow at our women's meeting which will be held at Ogboto-nta in the evening.

Ekechi: Okay o, I have heard you. I will be there, if *Chiokike* keeps us alive till tomorrow.

Next day

Kawawa: [as he was about to go and pick up his in-law for their journey to Lagos.] Nnanyi, please take these shekels for your snuff and the entertainment of your guests. I will send you some traditional attire by next month. Take good care of yourself and mama. Em! Mama told me that my sister Adaku will be getting married soon. Please, don"t bother yourself about the entertainment of the visitors, for I will send you enough shekels and food stuffs for that purpose next month.

Dikeoha: Thank you, my son. I"m now very relieved. God will bless you and your progeny.

Kawawa: Mama, please take this money for your meetings. Give these shekels to your daughters. I"m somewhat late. Goodbye papa, mama. God be with you all.

Ekechi: Thank you my beloved son, God will see you through in life. As you are taking care of us, so also will your offspring do unto you. Goodbye, my son.

Dikeoha & Ekechi:[as Kawawa zoomed, began to wave.] Bye! Bye!!Bye!!!

Ekechi: Nnanyi, *Chiokike* really blessed us. Kawawa has human milk flowing in his system.

Dikeoha: Ekechi, you know that a son must take after his father.

Ekechi: Nnanyi, are you saying that Kawawa took after you alone? Did I not bear him in my womb for nine months?

Dikeoha: Ekechi, listen. When a child is of good trait, he is a replica of the father but if the child is of bad trait, he resembles the mother. This is so because, the tendency of the woman having coition with another bloke, who may be of a bad trait can not be ruled out. Em! Ekechi, you can claim that your daughters took after you. After all, they are dark in complexion like you and Nwadinobi.

Ekechi: [as if weeping.] Nnanyi, is it because Nwadinobi is not of your loin? Why are you breaking my heart with harsh words?

Dikeoha: [striving to console his wife.] Ah! Ekechi, why are you weeping? I didn't mean to hurt you. I was just trying to respond to your questions. You see, there is an abyss between planting a seed and watering of the seed. I planted Kawawa and you watered him. Women are like fertile soil, where every farmer would like to plant one seed or the other. It is only when the seed germinates and grows that the soil will know whether she had accommodated a high-quality seed or an evil one.

Ekechi: [thoughtfully.] Ehn, so this singular error that culminated in the procreation of Nwadinobi will hunt me throughout the days of my life? Hmm! But, it was not my fault, if not for the tales from Upere to my parents, this sacrilegious act wouldn‟t have occurred.

Dikeoha: Ekechi! Ekechi!! Are you here with me? You seem to be mute, is anything the matter?

Ekechi: [battling to withhold her tears.] Nnanyi, it is well. I have to go to the backyard in order to harvest some cocoyam for the preparation of soup (ofe ede). I know you will like it.

Nwadinobi: [came in as Ekechi was still talking.] Papa! Mama! I greet you.

Dikeoha & Ekechi: [thoughtfully; talk of the devil, he is here now.] You are welcome. We hope all is well…

Nwadinobi: Hmm! All is not well o. I have to collect some shekels from you people.

Dikeoha: [furiously.] Hei! What do you call yourself, are you with your senses? What a guff? We expect you to send some money to us as your ageing parents; instead you are here demanding money from us.

Nwadinobi: Listen! Old man! You are merely recasting a scene in tales by moonlight. The shekels or your life. See this jack-knife, I will use it to stab you to death. You want me to starve to death. You don‟t appreciate my young household.

Dikeoha: [shivering at the sight of the jack-knife.] My son, but I established two oil mill factories for you.

Nwadinobi: Yes! What about that? The oil mills are not producing the listed results. My demands are far more above the income from the mills.

Dikeoha: My son, you know that we are ageing and can not effectively fend for ourselves, let alone another person.

Nwadinobi: Who is another person? Ooh! So, I"m no more your child? Mmm! You see, whatever you like utter, I will not leave this place without the sum of ten pounds.

Ekechi: My son, where do you expect us to go and get such an amount of money?

Nwadinobi: Look! Woman, stay out of this. This is bloke to bloke palaver. I will dish out your own bitter pills, after dealing with your husband.

Ekechi: Why are you talking to your father like that?

Nwadinobi: Who is my father? If actually he is my father, why should he allow me and my family to suffer privations?

Ekechi: Are you reflective at all? He laid a strong foundation for you. He sponsored your *Iwa-Akwa* ceremony and marriage. Two modern oil mills factories were established for you. What else do you want him to do for you? Is it how you are going to take care of us in our old age?

Nwadinobi: Hey! Woman! I have told you to stay clear. You people must give me the shekels, willy-nilly.

Dikeoha: [still shivering.] My son, where do you expect us to get such a huge amount of shekels?

Nwadinobi: Haba! Old man, don"t pretend as if you are bankrupt. For your information, I have the spiritual powers to see from a far distance. I saw the money given to you by that bastard you christened Kawawa. The money is right here with both of you.

Dikeoha: [being of good courage] Hey! Never you call my beloved son, Kawawa a bastard again o. Is it not a satire for a bonafide bastard and vagabond to call a licit child a bastard?

Nwadinobi: Kai! Kai!! Old man, are you referring to me as a bastard? Mm! I will teach you the lesson of your life, now.

Dikeoha: [while Nwadinobi was bashing them and struggling to take their money.] Eeh! Eeh!! Ewuoh! Ewuoh!! Umunna are you at home? We are dying ooh! Nwadinobi is killing us ooh!

Nwadinobi: [ere Umunna could come to their rescue, he had collected their shekel and fled away.] Hei! You old fool; this money will not be enough for me. I will come again soon, and if you refuse to give me money, I will sell-off your palm trees and domestic animals. I"m on my way to Kumirukiki.

Dikeoha & Ekechi:[still reeling in pain on the bare ground.] Why is it that Umunna refused to come to our rescue?

Ekechi: Mm! Nnanyi, it may be that Umunna did not hear our cry for help.

Dikeoha:[reflectively.] Ekechi, you are wrong, Umunna heard us. Umunna"s inaction is not unconnected with their hitherto stand on the status of Nwadinobi. To them, I"m reaping what I sowed, hence my refusal to take their advice.

Ekechi: Nnanyi, why are you not talking? Please, let"s get up and clean our body, so that we can look natty again and avoid tongue wagging.

Dikeoha: [as he was struggling to get up in pain, saw some people approaching.] Ekechi, see, Umunna are coming.

Ekechi: Nnanyi, don"t mind them. Why didn"t they come on time?

Umunna: [came into the compound.] Dikeoha! What is the matter? Why were you screaming like someone attacked by a ravenous lion?

Dikeoha: Mm! My people! What is more intriguing and powerful than the Cricket met her in the trench.

Umunna: What is it that met *Nte* in the hole?

Dikeoha: Hmm! My people, we know that it is not our custom for a man to wash his grubby loin-cloth in public. Eem! Eem!!

Ekechi: [not finding Dikeoha"s dilly-dallying comfortable, cut in.] The powerful thing that met us was Nwadinobi, our son. He mauled us and made away with our shekels.

Umunna: Chei! Chei!! We said it.

Ekechi: (cut in) Umunna! What did you say? I"m just telling you what transpired and you are here saying a different thing.

Dikeoha: Ekechi, please go inside, stop talking; for you will not understand. Let the men do the talking.

Umunna: [in the absence of Ekechi.] Dikeoha, in spite of your avoidable mistake, we are still your kinsmen. We will assist you to curb the excesses of that anathema. We have to leave you now.

Dikeoha: My people, I appreciate your concern, thanks a lot. Goodbye.

A year after

Dikeoha: Ekechi! Ekechi!!

Ekechi: Nnanyi here I am.

Dikeoha: [groping his fractured waist inflicted on him by Nwadinobi.] Ugh! Ekechi, this fractured waist will send me to an early grave o…

Ekechi: Nnanyi, *Chukwu ekwela ihe ojo*. God forbid. It would not kill you.

Dikeoha: Ekechi, now that Kawawa has decided to sponsor Ugwumba to acquire tailoring skills, I would suggest we get a wife for him.

Ekechi: Nnanyi, I"m behind you, hence we have married a wife for Nwadinobi and Kawawa.

Dikeoha: More especially, since it is our tradition for a poppa to sponsor his male children"s tying cloth and marriage ceremonies. It can"t be out of place for us to get a wife for Ugwumba. Em! Ekechi the ball is now on your court; do you have any damsel in mind?

Ekechi: Nnanyi, have you forgotten that we put some „kola nuts and shoots of young palm wine saplings into the vessel of drinking water of Akueze,
your chum"s daughter, when she was born? I often see her in the market. She has grown to womanhood.

Dikeoha: Oh! Oh!! Are you talking about the daughter of Osisiogu, the indefatigable wrestler of Rumuogu?

Ekechi: Yes, Nnanyi, she does assist me in the market most of the time. She is such a good girl. Her beauty is just like that of the butterfly.

Dikeoha: But, is she aware of the significance of the ritual carried out in her drinking vessel at birth?

Ekechi: Nnanyi, my chat with her indicates that her parents, especially her mother, had explained everything to her. She told me that she knows Ugwumba very well.

Dikeoha: Íyeá! You have already cleared the bush, let"s go and commence planting. Em! By the next *afor* market day, we shall go and see her parents, and kick off marriage rites.

Ekechi: Nnanyi, I thought we should have sent for Ugwumba before the commencement of the marital rites.

Dikeoha: Mm, it is not necessary for him to be around, besides he can"t abandon his apprenticeship. More so, since I"m still alive to represent him, his presence is needless for now.

Ekechi: Then, what will happen after paying the bride price?

Dikeoha: Em! Em!! Well, we shall give Akueze, the leverage to stay with her parents, until Ugwumba comes back from Lagos.

Ekechi: Nnanyi, you have spoken well. Please may I ask for your indulgence to go and see our daughter, Adaku? I learnt that she gave birth to a baby boy this morning.

Dikeoha: You are at liberty to leave. I know that you will soon zoom off again for another *omugwo*.

Ekechi: [humorously.] Nnanyi, don"t worry, I will allow you to go for this particular *omugwo* and experience what we usually encounter.

Dikeoha: Tufiakwa! It is an abomination for me to switch positions with you. May our progenitors not hear you reiterate such again o.

Ekechi: But Nnanyi, since you men recognize that *omugwo* is a feminine affair, why do you (men) raise your eyebrows at the sight of items brought home by women from *omugwo* mission?

Dikeoha:[beaming with smiles.] Ekechi, it is not that men are green-eyed monsters, as per goodies derived from *omugwo*. All the shenanigans are merely introspective expressions of excitement. After all, goodies from *omugwo* expeditions save the men the stress of purchasing new clothes and jewelry for their wives.

Ekechi: Nnanyi, you have won the debate; let me zoom off to Rumuokwe. I hope to see you by tomorrow morning.

Dikeoha: Em! Remember to extend my felicitation to our in-laws. Take care of yourself. Goodbye.

Scene 16

Dikeoha: [addressing his umunna two weeks after the introductory marital rituals of Akueze as tradition would demand.] Chai! Chai!! Chai!!! Umunna kwenu.

Umunna:Yáa!!

Dikeoha: Kwézuoñu o…

Umunna:Yáaa!!!

Dikeoha: My people, having presented kola nuts, I hope I"m at liberty to address you now?

Umunna:Yáaa!!! That is our tradition.

Dikeoha: It is an axiom in our land that he who does not have Umunna is like a walking corpse.

Umunna: You are right.

Dikeoha: Umunna is a bunch of broom that kills the fly at will while he who has no Umunna is the single broom that can never kill a fly.

Umunna: Dikeoha, accelerate; you are the son of your father.

Dikeoha: My kinsmen, in order not to waste your precious time with idiomatic expressions, I wish to present these kegs of palm wine, kola nuts and food as our custom would demand to inform you that, my son, Ugwumba would be getting married by the next *afor* market day; and as such, you are expected to accompany us to Rumuogu for the marriage ceremony proper. Thank you all.

Ezeudo: [the eldest man amongst the Umunna present.] Chai! Chai!! Chai!!! Umunna kweñu.

Umunna:Yáaa!!!

Ezeudo: Dikeoha! You are the real son of your father. On behalf of our Umunna, I thank you for the honour done to us. We are solidly behind you. My kinsmen, I hope your mind has been expressed?

Umunna: Yáaa! Ezeudo, you have spoken well. It is only a moron that would see a woman with full pregnancy and still inquire to know whether she is pregnant or not. Dikeoha is a son of the soil and deserves every support from us.

Dikeoha: My kinsmen, I appreciate you all for honouring my invitation and for accepting to accompany me to Rumuogu. I owe you hearty thanks for finding my food edible. Yes, a man does not invite his kinsmen for a feast because they're starving or do not have food in their homes but because it is a good thing for kinsmen to come together and make merry with each other; truly, anyone can see the moonlight from his abode but yet kinsmen like children gather at the village square to appreciate the moonlight and tell stories of interest to while away the night together with some kegs of palmwine. Verily, I have seen a man who prepared a delicious meal for his Umunna but none of them came to the feast, because of his demeanour towards them and at the end of the day, all the food was thrown to the dogs.

Ezeudo: You have spoken well. We appreciate your kind heartedness and respect for us. It is only a fool who does not acknowledge that, Umunna is an acute waist pain that should be treated with utmost care. Thank you very much. Em! I think we can leave now, since the message has been delivered. However, those who would like to stay behind and tackle the remaining wine should do so. Dikeoha, let me go and attend to my palm wine trees.

Dikeoha: Nnanyi Ezeudo, your comments are gratifying. *Chiokike* will guide and guard you. Yes! You will climb the palm trees and come down safely. Your guardian angel will never go to sleep. My kinsmen, I thank you once again for honouring my invitation.

Umunna: [as most of them were deserting.] Dikeoha, you have made our day with your moreish food and wine. We shall meet again on the forth-coming *afor* market day for the marital rites. Greet your wife for us. Be well.

Dikeoha: Be well too, my people, goodbye.

Ekechi: [after Umunna had left.] Nnanyi, how did it go with the menfolks?

Dikeoha: They were all excited and happy. The invitation was graciously accepted. My Umunna are solidly behind me. They expressed their felicity over your sumptuous meal. You are indeed a connoisseur in cookery.

Ekechi: The womenfolk acknowledged our hail-fellow-well-met demeanour. They eulogized our hospitality and entertainment and pledged to accompany us on that day. I gave them enough food and wine, far above what our rule stipulates. Em, didn"t you hear them singing and dancing?

Dikeoha: That is a palaver for womenfolk. Please, make sure that the oddments of meat are well dessicated for the entertainment of my visitors.

Ekechi: Nnanyi, your wish is my command. Let me go back to the kitchen and rearrange my utensils.

Dikeoha: [after Ekechi"s departure, began to ponder.] Hmm, so it is worthy for one to be on good terms with his Umunna? I"m perplexed at their response this evening. Does it mean that if I"m in the soup right now, Umunna will come to my rescue? But, have I not offended them by taking Nwadinobi as my son? Mmm! Well! Nwadinobi"s case is not for we mortals to consider, I hope *Chiokike* predestined it so. Well, let me go to my hut and relax my nerves after the day"s hectic engagements.

Scene 17

The next Afor Market Day

Ezeudo: [at Rumuogu, during Ugwumba"s marriage ceremony, assumed the matrix of mouthpiece for his kinsmen.] Cha! Cha!! Cha!!! People of Rumuogu kwenu.

Everybody: Yáaa!

Ezeudo: Kwézuoñu o.

Everybody: Yáaaa!

Ezeudo: [cleared his throat.] Hmm, my people, it is our tradition to feign not to know what a woman gave birth to, just to rhetorically enquire what she gave birth to. Yes, in line with this tradition of our progenitors, I wish to announce on behalf of my Umunna, that we have come to pluck on a beautiful flower which we saw in Osisiogu"s humble abode.

Nze Kamalu: [as a result of his old age, acted as the spokesman for the people of Rumuogu.] Cha! Cha!! Cha!!! People of Rumuoma, I greet you.

Everybody: Yáaa!

Nze Kamalu: Osisiogu, you have heard my friend, Ezeudo.

Osisiogu: Yes, Nnanyi.

Nze Kamalu: Do you have any flowers in your house?

Osisiogu: Nnanyi, I have so many human flowers in my house, but I don"t know the one they are seeking to pluck.

Nze Kamalu: Ezeudo my friend, you have heard from Osisiogu. Our people used to say that the hunter should name and identify the type of bird he desires to shoot, so that *Nkelu* (an inedible bird) should not disturb herself by flying away with great pain.

Ezeudo:[cleared his throat.] Hmm! Your message is clear. Our people do say that, if a proverb is used to explicate an issue to a man, and he expects the same to be interpreted to him like a toddler, it then indicates that the bride price paid on his mother is worthless. Yes, the name of the beautiful woman we are seeking her hand in marriage is Akueze.

Nze Kamalu: [pretending not to know.] Osisiogu, do you have any woman in your house bearing Akueze, as a name?

Osisiogu: Yes, Nnanyi, she is my third daughter.

Nze Kamalu: You should send for her.

Osisiogu:[calling his wife.] Urediya! Urediya!!

Urediya: Nnanyi, here I"m.

Osisiogu: Please, ask your daughter to come and greet our visitors, and show us her fiancé.

Akueze:[came in.] *Ndi Nnanyi ekélé m uñu* (my fathers, I greet you all).

Everybody: *Íyáa! Nwa oma* (Yes! Beautiful child). How are you?

Akueze: I"m fine.

Nze Kamalu: Akueze, my daughter, do you know anybody amongst our visitors here?

Akueze: Yes, Nnanyi. I know Nnanyi Dikeoha.

Nze Kamalu: Mm, my daughter! These people from Rumuoma said that they have come to seek your hand in marriage. What do you have to say? Should we accept their drinks?

Akueze: Yes, Nnanyi.

Nze Kamalu: Akueze! My daughter, for us to be cocksure of your acceptance, you should carry this cup of wine and present it to your would-be hubby. But if he is not available here now, you can give the wine to his poppa.

Akueze: Okay Nnanyi.

Nze Kamalu: Please! Okoh, give her some palm wine from the jar.

Akueze: [moving towards Dikeoha with the wine, knelt down and gave him the cup of wine.] Nnanyi, please take this cup of wine from me.

Dikeoha: [thanked her and sprayed some shekels on her.] My daughter, you have done well, get up.

Akueze: [got up, greeted everybody and left.] Nnanyi, ekélé kwà m unu òzò (My fathers, I greet you all once again).

Everybody: Thank you, our beautiful daughter, you have done well. We are proud of you.

Nze Kamalu: People of Rumuogu, Akueze has given us the green light to proceed with the marriage rituals. Now, we have the right to refer to the people of Rumuoma as our in-laws.

People of Rumuogu: Nnanyi, Nze Kamalu, you have spoken well. Your sonorous voice and words are like the red palm oil used to eat roasted yam.

Nze Kamalu: The marriage ceremony is hereby declared open. My in-laws! You can bring in all the traditional requirements for this occasion as contained in the list given to you by our scribe.

Ezeudo: [cleared his throat.] Our in-laws! We came here fully prepared. No stone shall be left unturned. Akubueze! Please, my son, organize other youths to assist you, bring in all the items we came here with.

Akubueze: [came in with the items.] Nnanyi, these are the items.

Ezeudo: Thank you, my son. You have done well. Em! My in-laws, on behalf of my kinsmen, I present all the items as contained in your list for inspection.

Nze Kamalu: [after inspection.] Hmm! My kinsmen, I think our in-laws left no stone unturned. We should appreciate their best endeavours.

People of Rumuogu: Our in-laws, you have done well, we greet you once again.

People of Rumuoma: We have accepted your greetings. We don"t encourage or accompany a pushover masquerade to the market square. Dikeoha is a man of his people and a biggie.

Ibika:[acting as a youth leader from Rumuogu, screamed with a croak voice.] Hmm, our in-laws, have you forgotten the need to „settle" the youths? We shielded and protected Akueze from the fangs of ruffians right from her tender age till date. Had it been we didn"t protect her, you wouldn"t have seen her for marriage.

Ezeudo: [cleared his throat.] My son, what you are demanding for is traditionally approved. Em, Dikeoha, please, go outside and reconcile with the youths.

Ibika: Nnanyi Ezeudo thanks for your understanding.

Nze Kamalu: Ibika! You can leave us now. Our in-laws, we have seen all that you presented to us but we are yet to deliberate on the bride price.

Ezeudo: [clears his throat.] Nze Kamalu, the onus is on you to present to us some of your elders to go out and deliberate on the bride price while the merriment and other aspects of the marital rites continue.

Nze Kamalu: Ezeudo, you have spoken my mind. Settlement of bride price is like dogs" play; each falling down for each other. I will give you some elders, who will thrash out the bride price with you.

Ezeudo: We are prepared for you people.

An Hour Later

Nze Okeke: [the leader of the bride price negotiation committee from Rumuogu.] Our in-laws, these are sixty broomsticks.

Ichie Ezindu: [leading the Rumuoma bride price negotiation team.] We have seen the broomsticks. Please take these.

Nze Okeke: [counted the broomsticks from Ichie Ezindu, they were thirty in number] Ichie take these.

Ichie Ezindu: [counted the broomsticks, they were forty-five in number] Nze Okeke, take these.

Nze Okeke: [counted the broomsticks and they were thirty-five in number] Ichie Ezindu, have these.

Ichie Ezindu: [counted the broomsticks and they were forty-two in number] Nze Okeke, take these.

Nze Okeke: [counted the broomsticks, they were thirty-seven sticks in number] Ichie Ezindu, take these.

Ichie Ezindu: [counted the broomsticks and they were forty in number. He consulted with his team] Nze Okeke, take these.

Nze Okeke: [counted the broomsticks and they were forty in number] Ichie! I think a deal has been struck at forty pounds, where we reach an equilibrium point.

Ichie Ezindu: Nze Okeke, you are right. Forty pounds is our meeting point. The bride price has been settled.

Nze Okeke: Em! Em!! My people, in the absence of any other business, can we rise and join other guests in the merriment galore out there?

All members: Nze Okeke, you have spoken well.

Ichie Ezindu: Em! Em!! Nze Okeke, you see, when announcing our accord, the sum of the bride price should not be publicized, hence, in our land, human beings are not sold like domestic animals.

Nze Okeke: Ichie Ezindu, you have just spoken my mind. Let"s go inside and join the entertainment train.

Nze Kamalu: [interrupts the hilarious ceremony.] Cha! Cha!! Cha!!! People of Rumuoma, kwenu.

Everybody: Yáaa!

Nze Kamalu: Cha! Cha!! Cha!!! People of Rumuogu, kwenu.

Everybody: Yáaa!

Nze Kamalu: Kwézuonu.

Everybody: Yáaa!

Nze Kamalu: [clears his throat.] Hmm! I wish to use this opportunity to inform you that our bride price negotiation teams are back. May I call on Nze Okeke to acquaint us, how it went?

Nze Okeke: My people, all other protocols observed. Em! Em!! I have the pleasure to tell you that the negotiation went fine. As you are all aware, bride price is not publicized. Those who are directly concerned will be briefed in due course. Cha! Cha!! Cha!!! Ohananweze kwenu.

Everybody: Yáa!

Nze Okeke: Kwézuonu.

Everybody: Yáaa!!!

Nze Kamalu: Ohananweze (everybody), you have heard it all from the horse"s mouth that the transaction went on cordially. Ehm! With the bride price being settled, the marital rituals have been completed, merriment should continue, those who want to leave can do so peacefully. Cha! Cha! Cha!!! *Igbo bu Igbo kwézuonu.*

Everybody: Yáaa!

Ezeudo: [cleared his throat.] Cha! Cha!! Cha!!! People of Rumuogu, kwenu.

Everybody: Yáaa!

Ezeudo: Cha! Cha!! Cha!!! People of Rumuoma kwénu.

Everybody: Yáaa!

Ezeudo: Kwézuonu.

Everybody: Yáaa!

Ezeudo: [clears his throat once more.] Em!! Ohananweze; with the power bestowed on me by my kinsmen, I wish to thank everyone here present and especially our in-laws, the people of

Rumuogu for their understanding and appreciation of our endeavours. This palsy-walsy is a sign of good things to come. As for Osisiogu and his immediate family, we appreciate their humble profile and support throughout the marriage ritual sessions. Hmm! We still have more bachelors in our community and Akueze"s marriage will not be the last, as we shall come again. On this note, I wish to announce our plea to leave, since it is dark already and some of us have to attend to our palm trees this evening. Thank you all.

Nze Kamalu: [clears his throat.] Ezeudo, my friend, you have spoken well. I hope these youngsters are learning from you… As you can see, with our age, our days are numbered. Hmm, that"s by the way. Ohananweze! On behalf of my Umunna from Rumuogu, I wish to thank our in-laws for their humility and perseverance throughout the duration of the marital rituals. I wish them journey mercies. Our daughter, Akueze, shall procreate male and female children for her husband. Dikeoha"s descendants shall be multiplied through her. *Chiokike* will provide for all your needs. Goodbye.

Everybody: Íséé o o!! Nze! You have spoken well.

PHASE THREE

The Sacrilege

Nwadinobi: After the marriage ceremony of Akueze, her final change of home was tarried because her hubby, Ugwumba was yet to arrive from Lagos.

During this period of interregnum, Nwadinobi"s friend, Osuji, took him to visit his fiancée. On getting to their destination, after a delightful treat, the green-eyed monster in Nwadinobi evoked, and he began to ponder on how to take the nubile from his friend. After the visit, Nwadinobi went behind his friend to see and deceived the maiden with sweet talks. He embarked on a campaign of calumny against his chum. He employed the strategy of an impostor to lure the damsel into marriage. Having accepted to marry him, Nwadinobi was faced with financial constraints. He, eventually, thought out something strange in human history. Thus, he went to his father (Dikeoha) and told him incredible and sordid stories about Akueze. He suggested that they should hurry and collect the bride price. He also intimated his father that he had found a very good and homely damsel for his younger brother (Ugwumba). Initially, Dikeoha refused to oblige to his request, and strived to apprise Nwadinobi, about the cordial relationship existing between the two families. But Nwadinobi, recalcitrantly, threatened to bring down thunder and hail stone if his ex cathedra pronouncement is not adhered to. Out of intimidation, Dikeoha allowed him to go for the bride price. After retrieving the bride price, Nwadinobi made arrangements and commenced marriage proceedings on the new girl, Mgbafor. He informed the whole „Umunna", especially members of his younger brother"s age-grade that he was embarking on the marital process on behalf of Ugwumba. The process was sped up. However, before the final marriage rites, the damsel was already pregnant for him, thus, the emergence of his second wife. Verily, mouth and tongue began to wag, but for the shameless crook, all these meant nothing to him. Dikeoha and Ekechi, his parents, nearly gave up the ghost to heart attack. Ugh! What a shame?

Act Three

Scene 1

Osuji: [A month after the marriage of Akueze at Nwadinobi‟s place.] Nwadinobi, you know we have been childhood friends.

Nwadinobi: Yes! I know that even the marines are aware of this fact. Is anything the matter?

Osuji: You see, I have been telling you of one damsel, whom I wish to marry since my father couldn‟t marry for me in time as your father did for you, as a result of his untimely demise.

Nwadinobi: Yes! What about her?

Osuji:[being skeptical of Nwadinobi.] Hmm! Well! Em! Em!! Em!!!

Nwadinobi: Osuji! Osuji!! When did you become a stammerer? I"m suspecting this sudden stuttering of yours o.

Osuji: [strived to be of good courage and left all to fate.] Hmm! There is nothing to worry about, Nwadinobi. You see, as my bosom buddy, I would like you to accompany me to my fiancée"s abode this evening.

Nwadinobi: Mm! Where is the place? Is it far from our village? You are aware that we are now in harmattan season.

Osuji: What is wrong with harmattan? It is not tempestuous in our region.

Nwadinobi: [amusingly.] Em! My friend, you will not understand until you get married. The season is so demanding on us, married men.

Osuji: Nwadinobi! Are you making a mockery of me? Chei! Wonders shall never end. If not for the benevolence of your father, it would have taken you a century to get married. Concisely, you would have remained an *okèokporo* (perpetual bachelor). If I may ask, how would you have raised money to marry? Right now, you can"t even manage the Oil Mill factories established for you by Nnanyi Dikeoha. Let me put it to you that, had it been, I had such opportunities as you did, I would have been one of the richest men in this community.

Nwadinobi: Em! Osuji, let"s forget about our parents for now. Can we start going to your fiancée„s place?

Osuji: Ehen! Now you are talking like a rational adult. Let"s zoom off.

Nwadinobi: Lest I forget, where are we heading to?

Osuji: [while on the way to his fiancée"s place.] Our destination is Rumuabali.

Nwadinobi: Okay! That‟s right. I have a few of my friends over there. We will soon get there. It is contiguous to our village.

Osuji: [at his fiancée‟s abode striving to introduce Nwadinobi.] Em! Em!! Mgbafor, this is Nwadinobi, my bosom friend. Nwadinobi, this is Mgbafor my fiancée.

Mgbafor: Nnanyi, you are welcome.

Nwadinobi:Yáa, beautiful girl, how are you?

Mgbafor: I‟m fine.

Osuji: Mgbafor, where are your parents?

Mgbafor: They went for our community‟s gathering at Mgboto-Ukwu square.

Osuji: Well! Mgbafor, we shall be going now, please take these shekels for your make-up and other needs.

Mgbafor: Thank you, Nnanyi. I‟m grateful. I will tell my parents that you came. Goodbye.

Osuji & Nwadinobi: Goodbye. Take care of yourself.

Nwadinobi: [on their way home.] Osuji, this girl is very beautiful o. How did you trap her into accepting your marriage proposal?

Osuji: [while smiling.] Nwadinobi! Why are you so inquisitive about my betrothed?

Nwadinobi: Haba! Osu-nwanna...! Are we not friends again? Aren't I supposed to know some details about your betrothed?

Osuji: Hmm! Since you insist, I met her at Etekah stream. You see, as I was making a crossover to the other side of the stream, she beckoned on me to assist her, lift-up her water pot to her head. It was during that process and beyond that one thing led to the other.

Nwadinobi: Osuji, my brother! You are really a lucky man. This damsel must be the hardworking type.

Osuji: Ah, yes o, she is a complete workaholic; her domestic chore is her whole life. If she is not in the farm, she is fetching water or fire wood for her mother or grandmother. She is always at the Etekah stream, every morning and evening fetching water or laundering.

Nwadinobi: [looking morose, and pondering.] Hmmn! Osuji! You are finished. I have to see this nubile tomorrow evening at Etekah stream as you have foolishly revealed. How can you have this elegant damsel for yourself? Stupid short man!

Osuji: Nwadinobi! Why are you looking gloomy and mute? Is anything the matter?

Nwadinobi: Osu-mimi! You see, I was just pondering over my family. As you can see, it is getting dark.

Osuji: My dear, we are already at home. I wish to thank you for accompanying me to my would-be in-law"s place.

Nwadinobi: Osu-mimi! Osu-nwanna! Please, don"t mention that, why are we friends? I hope to see you tomorrow. Goodbye.

Scene 2

Nwadinobi: [the next day at the Etekah stream with Mgbafor, Osuji"s betrothed.] Mgbafor, how are you?

Mgbafor:I"m fine, Nnanyi. How about your friend, Osuji?

Nwadinobi: [on a campaign of calumny.] Hmm! Mgbafor! You wouldn"t believe that, Osuji did not go home with me yesterday o.

Mgbafor: What happened? Is he alright? Oh, my God!

Nwadinobi: Listen! Don"t bother yourself. I"m here to tell you to be wary. Why should you waste your precious time and affection on a bloke, who does not appreciate you?

Mgbafor: [cut in, curiously.] What are you insinuating? Are you saying that Osuji is not what he showcases himself to be?

Nwadinobi: Em! Em! Although this is difficult to say.

Mgbafor: [cut in]. What is it? Please say it now.

Nwadinobi: Well, since you insist, this is what I have to say. You see, on our way home yesterday, Osuji went to sleep the night with *Mgborie*, another girl, whom he also promised to marry.

Mgbafor: Nnanyi, this is hard to chew. I can"t believe your story. This is a shaggy-dog tale.

Nwadinobi: [cynically.] Mgbafor! The earlier you start believing the revelation, the better for you.

Mgbafor: [while weeping.] But he told me that he loves me and that I'm the only woman in his life.

Nwadinobi: Ah! Women! You are so gullible to sweet nothings. Let me apprise you, Osuji"s middle name is lie while falsehood is his favorite pastime.

Mgbafor: Are you saying that Osuji, my beau has been lying to me all these while?

Nwadinobi: He has not only been lying to you, he has been working towards ruining your life. You see, his tongue is like a sharp razor, working deceitfully. The words of his mouth are smoother than butter and softer than oil, yet they harbour swords. I have known Osuji for ages, he cherishes evil more than good, and lies more than honesty.

Mgbafor: [cut in.] Ehn! Nnanyi, since you are aware that Osuji is the Old Nick reincarnate, why have you been hobnobbing with him, to the extent of accompanying him to my place?

Nwadinobi: [cut in.] That is it! The strategy is camouflage. You see, I deliberately came with him to your place in order to save you from his fangs. He had jilted an avalanche of damsels in the past. Verily, our companionship went sour, when he impregnated one of his far cousins; and he was made to dance round the market square in nude as a purification ritual.

Mgbafor: Chei! Chei!! Chei!!! God! Ehn! So, Osuji had concealed all these from me. Nnanyi, *Chiokike* will be with you. What can I do to reward you for all the information?

Nwadinobi: [gladdened in his heart.] Mgbafor! I know you don"t deserve people like Osuji who are callous with women. You need good and amiable men like us, who care for women, as their nature demands.

Mgbafor: Thanks for your concern, Nnanyi. But I still don"t know how to reward you for rescuing me from the claws of Osuji?

Nwadinobi: [pawkily.] Ah! How to reward me is not far-fetched. Yes! You can reward me in different ways, for instance, accepting to be my wife.

Mgbafor: Ah! Ah!! Nnanyi, but you are married.

Nwadinobi: Hmm! You see, the woman I"m staying with was married by my parents, ignorantly. Now, I want to make my own choice, and sponsor my own marriage rites.

Mgbafor: Em! Nnanyi, I must confess, your proposal is a hard nut to crack; however, I will ponder over it.

Nwadinobi: [sentienting green light.] Mgbafor! Listen to a clarion call for affection. You should not only ponder over my gold-dust proposal, but embrace the same with both arms. I will see you tomorrow for a reply. As you know, anything that concerns fresh meat deserves ultimate urgency.

Mgbafor: But Nnanyi, who really are you? Who is your father?

Nwadinobi: Ehn! Mgbafor! You are really a humdinger. These posers of yours are in order. Well! My father is Dikeoha.

Mgbafor: [cut in.] Are you saying that Dikeoha, the popular herbal doctor, is your father?

Nwadinobi: Yes, I"m his first son. Em! Do you know him?

Mgbafor: Well! Not really but my mother does eulogize his sterling qualities. I learnt that Dikeoha is huge and fair in complexion but how come you are dark in complexion?

Nwadinobi: You see, I took after my mother in complexion.

Mgbafor: Alright! I can see. We shall see tomorrow.

Nwadinobi: Mgbafor! Now that you have known my family background, what stops you from giving a reply to my petition right here? You see, I want to commence preparations for our marriage rites immediately.

Mgbafor: [beaming with smiles.] Nnanyi, why are you in so much of a hurry? Even if I can‟t say it out loud, can‟t you read the meaning to my demeanour?

Nwadinobi: I can understand your moves and reactions, but I wanted to be sure that all is well with my proposal. Goodbye.

Mgbafor: Goodbye, Nnanyi, greet your family for me.

Nwadinobi: [on his way home, began to soliloquize.] Ehn! Now that I have taken over this beautiful girl from Osuji, the only onerous task confronting me now is how to raise some shekels for the marital rites. I‟m stony-broke. What am I going to do now? Oh! Yes! That‟s it. I have to go to my father right now and compel him to retrieve the bride price paid on Ugwumba‟s wife; thereafter, I will use the shekels to settle Mgbafor‟s marital rites.

Osuji: [after a few moments of Nwadinobi‟s exit, came to Mgbafor‟s abode.] Mgbafor! Mgbafor!!

Mgbafor: [looked daggers at Osuji, as she came out of the hut.] Hei! What is that your unholy name? What do you want here? Son of a bitch, I don‟t want to see you here again. I hope you have gotten the message into your fucking skull? You incurable Casanova.

Osuji: Mgbafor! I‟m lost. What is going on here? What is the matter? Please, be rational and tell me what is amiss.

Mgbafor: Yes! All your hocus-pocus and lies had been uncovered. Chei! I didn‟t even know that, you impregnated your own cousin. You are a shameless bastard. Now get out of this place before I crush your hydra-head. Stupid dwarf.

Osuji: Mgbafor, this is hard to chew. Since you have laid grievous allegations against me without allowing me the scintilla opportunity to defend myself, I beg to leave. But before I leave, I would like you to be rational by telling me who mounted this campaign of calumny against me.

Mgbafor: What do you mean by rational? Hei! You better desert now before you lose your thick skull. You niwit! I will never reveal the source of my information to you. Ugh! Exit from here now, you „short engine".

Osuji: [as he was deserting.] *Chiokike* will judge you and I. Whoever that put asunder to our relationship will exist to regret such action.

Scene 3
A week later

Nwadinobi: [striving to impel Dikeoha to retrieve Akueze"s bride price. He told unthinkable lies against the young maiden.] Em! Nnanyi, I want you to go and retrieve the bride price paid on Akueze.

Dikeoha: Chei! Tufiakwa! May our progenitors forbid it! This is sacrilegious. Hmm! If I may ask, what prompted you to make such an unfathomable suggestion?

Nwadinobi: Nnanyi, I do see Akueze, sleep around. As you know, such a lascivious and wayward woman is susceptible to contamination of our family with bastards. More so, she would turn Ugwumba into a henpecked husband.
In the interim, I have found a well-behaved damsel for Ugwumba. So let"s make haste while the sun shines and retrieve the bride price.

Dikeoha: [recast the historical relationship between the two families and refused to oblige Nwadinobi"s request.] Hei! Listen! I have known Osisiogu"s family for ages. Any shebang that will strain our relationship is forbidden. Your request is against our tradition. If a man decides to back out of a marital contract, he should tarry until the jilted woman is remarried before he could retrieve the hitherto bride price.

Nwadinobi: Aha! I"m zooming off to Rumuogu to apprise Osisiogu to allow his daughter to remarry; we are no longer interested in her.

Dikeoha: Hei! I forbid you! Never try that. You are asking for the wrath of our ancestors on you.

Nwadinobi: Look! Oldster! Stay out of this. Come hell or high water, I will go to Rumuogu to deliver the message. Anyone who attempts to scuttle my plans will be crushed. I have warned you, stay away. I"m on my way to Osisiogu"s abode.

Dikeoha: [in a sober reflective mood.] Hmmmm! The worst of this criminal is yet to come! This is an abominable act, afterall, my son Ugwumba and I didn't complain. Ugh! What is wrong with this greedy idiot? My instincts tell me, he is up to something strange in human history.

Scene 4

Nwadinobi: [at Osisiogu"s home.] Nnanyi, I have come to inform you that your daughter, Akueze, is at liberty to remarry. My brother, Ugwumba, is no longer interested in her.

Osisiogu: [deeply touched by the turn of events.] Hmn! This meat is not for me alone to chew. My umunna has to hear this and bear witness. (calling his son) Ekwendu! Ekwendu!!

Ekwendu: Nnanyi, here I"m.

Osisiogu: Go to the houses of our kinsmen, those that are still at home, ask them to come over to my house quickly. Tell them that what is more powerful than *Nte* met her in the trench.

Ekwendu: [zoomed off, and came back in a jiffy.] Nnanyi, I met about twelve elders, they are coming behind me.

Umunna: [came in as Ekwendu was still talking.] Osisiogu! What is the matter? Why send such a message as if the sacrilegious is about to happen?

Osisiogu: Mmm! something more than sacrilege is in the offing. Ehn! Nwadinobi, can you repeat what you told me earlier in the presence of my umunna?

Nwadinobi: This is not the right time for entreaties. The message is clear and simple. You should allow your daughter, Akueze to remarry. We are no longer interested in her.

Umunna: What are your reasons? Is your father aware of this? We are going to send emissaries to him to uncover the mystery behind this abominable act.

Nwadinobi: This is our household decision. I have to personally deliver the message as the heir apparent. As you may be aware, Caesar"s verdict is never challenged.

Umunna: Hei! Besides your position as the first son, your father must have something to tell us on this issue. In the interim, our emissaries shall be at your home tomorrow morning.

Nwadinobi: Look! We don"t want to see anybody; just allow your daughter to remarry and return our bride price, period. I"m going. But let me warn! Anybody coming to our house as an emissary is doing so at his own peril. Good day.

Umunna: [as Nwadinobi exit.] Chei! Tufiakwa! What sort of human being is this? He is not like Dikeoha and the other offsprings, who are of lily-white character.

Osisiogu: Mm! my kinsmen, you should not bother yourself about him. I learnt from a reliable source that he is not the product of Dikeoha"s loin. His biological father is that notorious criminal from Rumuazi.

Umunna: [chorused.] Do you mean Osueke?

Osisiogu: You are right.

Umunna: [while reeling in laughter.] What a gruffy character? True! Blood never tells lies. We should not mind that bastard o.

Ibu: [one of the Umunna.] Em! Let us give Dikeoha and his son, Ugwumba two months grace to come and pick up Akueze to their home. But if they refuse to show up, our daughter, Akueze should be allowed to remarry.

Umunna: Ibu, you have spoken wisely. That is our stand.

Osisiogu: Umunna, I"m extremely sorry for bothering you with my problem. Please, take these kola nuts to your homes since our discussions disrupted our traditional presentation of kola nuts.

Umunna: Ah! Osisiogu you should not worry yourself. We are your Umunna. Thank you for the kola nuts. Goodbye.

Osisiogu: [as he was escorting his Umunna.] Goodbye, my kinsmen. I will see you in the evening at Mgboto-Ukwu, the meeting square. Ekwendu! Ekwendu!! Ekwendu!! Please! Come and clear this place.

Scene 5

Two months after

Nwadinobi: [at Osisiogu"s abode.] Osisiogu! I have come to retrieve the bride price, hence the marriage of Akueze to another man.

Osisiogu: You see, the money is available but my kinsmen have to witness the handover. Ah! Osondu, Uguru, Ikoro, Ojii, Orji, Ebebe, you are welcome. I was about sending for you people. Mm! please, we shall eat kola nuts later. Em! Em!! This man here has come to retrieve the bride price, since Akueze has been remarried.

Umunna: Okay, Osisiogu, you have spoken well, please, give that money to Osondu to hand over the same to Nwadinobi.

Osondu: Ehn! Em! Nwadinobi! This is the bride price, have it and leave us alone.

Nwadinobi: You have done the right thing, although belated. Goodbye.

Umunna: [after the exit of Nwadinobi.] You see, we learnt that his father was not in support of this action, but for the fact that he threatened to eliminate the old man, he stayed out of his way. Dikeoha is a good man; he can never back such an abominable action.

Osisiogu: My people, this may be a blessing in disguise o. Who knows what would have happened to my daughter with his presence in Dikeoha"s family? I learnt that he started exhibiting rascality at the age of four. It is only his demise that could put an end to his greedy traits.

Umunna: Osisiogu, keep fit. Let"s go and attend to our palm trees for evening wine. Goodbye.

Osisiogu: *Umunna unu emeela nke oma.* (My kinsmen, you have done well). Greet your families for me, bye, bye oo.

Scene 6

Two days later

Nwadinobi: [addressed Ugwumba"s age mates before going to carry out the marital rites of Mgbafor at Rumuabali.] Ehn! My younger brothers! I summoned you all here to secure your participation in these marriage rituals, since the maiden is being married to one of your age grade (Ikemba age grade) members, who are fortunately my younger brother, Ugwumba, who is still in Lagos.

Ikemba age grade: Nnanyi, we will participate fully because Ugwumba is a staunch member of our age grade. But we hope what happened to Akueze will not repeat itself?

Nwadinobi: Such a thing will never happen again, Mgbafor is not as wayward as Akueze. Please, let"s proceed; you know the elders are already on their way.

Ikemba age grade: O yea! Let"s go. We are going to show the people of Rumuabali that the people of Rumuoma does not lack vibrant youths.

Obidike: [after the marital rites at Rumuabali.] Our in-laws, having fulfilled all righteousness, we beg to leave for the journey ahead of us is quite a distance. More importantly, most of us have to attend to our palm trees this evening.

Iwuala: [acting as the spokesman of the people of Rumuabali.] Our in-laws, on behalf of my kinsmen, I wish you all journey mercies. I hope our daughter"s hubby will soon come back from Lagos as you said. Goodbye.

Dikeoha: [on their way home, talking to Obidike and Nwadinobi.] Em! Did both of you observed that virtually all our elderly Umunna did not show up for this occasion?

Obidike: Nnanyi, you observed right. Even our in-laws did not come out en masse. What could have been responsible for such spontaneous actions?

Dikeoha: Ugh! Obidike! I don"t blame any of them. No right thinking elder will overlook what happened to Akueze and embrace another marriage ritual by the same family who made mockery of them at Rumuogu. I know that shameful act will see me to the grave. I also learned that Mgbafor was Osuji"s betrothed. That was why most of the people of Rumuabali refused to embrace the occasion. Chei! *Chiokike!* What have I done wrong? Save me o.

Nwadinobi: Em! Em!! Yes! Let them not come. We have carried out the marital rites, so their presence is insignificant.

Obidike: Nnanyi Dikeoha, in order to avoid repetition, you have to send for Ugwumba immediately to come home and take over his wife.

Nwadinobi: (Looking morose and reflective) Ehn! Chei! Look at these nincompoops. So they think that I, Nwadinobi, will waste my precious time and energy to marry a wife for another man? *Ndi Iberibe* (fools), they don"t even know that Mgbafor is almost two months pregnant.

Obidike: Nwadinobi! Nwadinobi!! Are you here with us? Did you hear what I said? Make sure you tell your brother, Ugwumba to come back on time and take over his possession, Mgbafor.

Nwadinobi: [cynically.] I have heard you; your words are like salt. I will do precisely what you said.

Obidike: Nwadinobi, I appreciate your brotherly affection. Nnanyi Dikeoha, please, take heart, it shall be well. In the interim, I have to leave for my house. I have to visit some of my palm wine trees before it's dark. Goodbye, *ká chi bóó.*

Dikeoha: Obidike, my brother, thank you for the support and soothing words. Em! See you tomorrow at the marriage ceremony of Ukachi"s daughter.

Obidike: Okay, Nnanyi.

Scene 7

Kawawa: [at Lagos, one month after the marital rite of Mgbafor.] Ugwumba! Ugwumba!!

Ugwumba: Here I"m brother.

Kawawa: You see, I will be traveling to the village this morning to see the extent of work at my new site as being supervised by our brother, Nwadinobi. Take care of everybody. I don"t intend to stay long.

Ugwumba: Okay, brother, I wish you a hitch-free journey. *Chidube gi, Ijeoma* (may the Lord lead you, safe journey).

Kawawa: *Íséé o.* (Amen o.)

Scene 8

Kawawa: [at home.] Nnanyi, since I came back I have not seen my mother. Where is she?

Dikeoha: Hmm! Your mother had a heart attack as a result of what Nwadinobi did. Meanwhile, she is receiving treatment at your maternal home.

Kawawa: What did he do? Did he manhandle her?

Dikeoha: My son, it is hard to chew. You see, after forcefully aborting Akueze"s marriage to Ugwumba, he told us that he had seen a good maiden for Ugwumba at Rumuabali. We went there and performed the marriage rites only to discover later that she was already pregnant and Nwadinobi was responsible.

Kawawa: Ugh! What a shameful act? What about the house, which I sent a huge shekels to him to build for me?

Dikeoha: The building is still as you left it; no single brick has been added. The Adder can never discard its toga. I learnt he uses the shekels to prepare charms, so that you will not remember home again.

Kawawa: Nnanyi! I will strangle him on sight.

Dikeoha: My son, I forbid you, do not do such a thing. Just leave him alone, *Chiokike* will take control. In the interim, you can send your younger brother, Ugwumba to supervise the building project for you. I wish that cursed dog, Nwadinobi, would remain quiet and avoid the wrath of our progenitors.

Kawawa: Nnanyi, I have heard you. I wish to go and see mama this evening. I intend to pass the night over there. I shall be leaving for Lagos in two day"s time.

Dikeoha: I appreciate you, my son. God will always guard and guide you. You are the beginning of my youth. You are my citadel and strength.

Kawawa: Mm! Nnanyi, I"m aware of all the ill-treatment you and mama have been receiving from Nwadinobi. How he used to intimidate you and collect all the shekels and other items which I sent to you.

Dikeoha: Hmm! My son, you should not bother yourself much about that. He is busy making his grave, because when we are no more, what will he depend upon?

Kawawa: Look! If your existence means nothing to him, it means a lot to us. I will not take it lightly with him, if his rascality on you persists. Enough of this horseshit, you know! Nnanyi, I have to zoom off to my maternal home now. We shall deliberate on more important issues affecting the family on my return, tomorrow. Till then, remain blessed.

Dikeoha: My son, *Chiokike* will see you through this trip. Greet your mother for me.

The Next Day

Kawawa: [came back from his maternal home, Rumuodara with his mother, Ekechi.] Nnanyi! Nnanyi!!

Dikeoha: Who is calling? Wait a minute. Ah! My son, so you came back with your mother? Ekechi, how are you recuperating?

Ekechi: Nnanyi, the sickness left me the instant I saw my son. At least, I have someone on whom I can fall back on, in times of distress.

Kawawa: Mama, you are right. What both of you deserve now, at this age are support and affection, not intimidation and heart breaking. You are to be treated like babies. Please, mama, go inside and have some refreshment, while I stay with papa for some chat.

Ekechi: You have spoken well, my son. See you later.

Kawawa: [after the exit of Ekechi.] Nnanyi, as you said earlier, I will send Ugwumba back home by next month, to supervise the building project, as adjusted to suit my present financial strength, since Nwadinobi had wasted lots of resources meant for the project.

Dikeoha: Em, please, my son, don"t tell your brother, Ugwumba about the pregnancy of Mgbafor. I know the news will devastate him. I prefer him to come home and see things for himself.

Kawawa: Nnanyi, your words are always sagacious. I will do as you said. Please, permit me to go inside to relax my nerves as against tomorrow"s journey.

Dikeoha: You are at liberty my son. Lagos is a pretty far distance. You need enough rest this evening.

The Next Day

Kawawa: [in the morning as he was about to zoom off to Lagos.] Nnanyi, please take this money for your various contributions and entertainment of your guests. Ehn! Mama, manage these shekels for your upkeep and meetings. I will send some money to you through Ugwumba who will be coming home by next month. You people should remain blessed. Goodbye.

Dikeoha & Ekechi: You have done well our son. God will be with you throughout your journey. Goodbye!

Scene 9

A month later

Ugwumba: [at home in the village.] Nnanyi, since I came back, two days ago, you have not said anything about the damsel whom you said you were marrying for me.

Dikeoha: My son, it is hard to chew. You see, when water fills the mouth of a frog, she finds it clumsy to croak.

Ugwumba: Nnanyi, come off your shell and elucidate on the issue raised by me. You married wives for my brothers, why should my case be heard as tales by moonlight? Mm! What is it that is hard to chew?

Dikeoha: Please! I"m in great pain right now. I have a deep cut in my heart. Just go outside and enquire from members of your age grade what happened. I hope they will be in a better position to tell you what we went through in the last two months.

Ugwumba: [went out to see Uzoma, his bosom chum.] *Di anyi* (my mate)! What is it that happened these past months, that my father directed me to my age mates for an explanation?

Uzoma: Well! Umh! It"s all about your wife o. You see, your father married Akueze for you; after elaborate marital rituals, your brother, Nwadinobi, aborted the marriage. As if that was not enough crime, after the marriage of Mgbafor on your behalf, Nwadinobi impregnated and coveted her. This sacrilegious act left your parents in great shame and pain. However, *di anyi*, I will admonish you to leave everything to God. His end will definitely be disastrous.

Ugwumba: *Di anyi*, I"m not surprised, after what we passed through in his hand at Kumirukiki. I will accept it as my fate. I only pray that this man should not send our parents to an early grave.

Uzoma: *Di anyi*, please, let"s leave that evil man alone and talk about some other issues that are crucial to our lives. Ehen! We are to attend the marriage ceremony of our age grade"s public relations officer, Ukandu, in the evening of tomorrow at Rumuariam.

Ugwumba: Okay, I have heard you. Mm, please, I would like you to assist me in the supervision of my brother, Kawawa"s building. You see, all the shekels sent to Nwadinobi for this purpose were squandered, so he mandated me to supervise the adjusted building plan. In the interim, let me go and carry out some work at home.

Uzoma: *Di anyi*, be rest assured, I"m always at Kawawa"s services. He is an affable and benevolent kinsman. We shall see tomorrow for the marriage ceremony. Good bye.

Scene 10

Three months after

Ugwumba: Nnanyi, now that my refresher course with Amadi‟s fashion house is over, I wish to be a journeyman tailor, in order to raise some shekels and establish my own workshop.

Dikeoha: My son, I can only sympathize with your plight, since I‟m not sturdy enough to assist you. Hmm, you will have my blessings in whatever venture you delve into. Meanwhile, I will advise you to join any trustworthy *ogbo* (thrift group).

Ugwumba: Nnanyi, I understand and appreciate your concern, and also your inability to assist me financially. My prayer to *Chiokike* is for your protection and long life.

Okonkwo: [came in as Ugwumba and Dikeoha were discussing.] Nnanyi Dikeoha, I greet you.

Dikeoha: Yáa! You are welcome. How about your household?

Okonkwo: Nnanyi, they were fine, when I left home.

Ugwumba: Nnanyi Okonkwo, I greet you.

Okonkwo: Īyáa, my brother. How are you managing with your job?

Ugwumba: Nnanyi, I‟m still striving to put things together.

Okonkwo: Mm! Why not join my *ogbo* (thrift institution)? I will make sure you receive an overdraft as soon as possible, to enable you to purchase your sewing machines and other materials. And more importantly to open a standard workshop.

Ugwumba: Uuh! Nnanyi, I‟m convinced that it is my *chi* (guardian angel) that directed you here this evening. I will definitely join your *ogbo* in the next two *orie* market days.

Dikeoha: Okonkwo, my son, you have always been your brother"s keeper. What an unfathomable inspiration? Well! I"m not surprised to see your concern for the plight of others. Your benevolency comes from *Chiokike*. My supplication is that God should bless you plentifully and grant you long life.

Okonkwo: *Íséé o*! Nnanyi, actually, I came to see how you are recuperating from your ill-health?

Dikeoha: My son, Okonkwo, you have done well. I"m still regaining my health gradually. You know the trauma which I passed through in the hands of Nwadinobi, is still lingering. Mm! I know this will lead me to my grave.

Okonkwo: Nnanyi, *Chiokike* will heal you very soon. You can"t desert us so soon to join your ancestors. We still need a lot more to learn from you. Em! Ugwumba, ensure that you keep to your words to join the *ogbo*. I have to exit now. Goodbye, Nnanyi.

Dikeoha & Ugwumba: Goodbye.

Scene 11
Three months later

Okonkwo: [at his abode with Ugwumba.] Ehn! Ugwumba, this is the loan I promised to give you, as a member of the *ogbo* group. You can now establish a workshop of your own. I wish you godspeed.

Ugwumba: Thank you, Nnanyi Okonkwo; Chukwu (God) will reward you abundantly for your kind-heartedness. Em…let me go home and organize myself for the arduous task ahead.

Okonkwo: Okay, my brother, make haste while the sun is still shining. You ought to purchase a sewing machine first. This will, however, take you to Onitsha market.

Ugwumba: I appreciate your concern and direction. I will see you after my trip to Onitsha tomorrow, goodbye.

Okonkwo: Go well, my brother, I wish you successful haggling and journey mercies.

Scene 12

Ugwumba: [at home in the evening.] Brother Nwadinobi, would you please accompany me to Onitsha market tomorrow to purchase a sewing machine and other items?

Nwadinobi: Em! If you can pay for my transportation and entertainment bills, and provide some pocket money for me, I will accompany you.

Ugwumba: Ugh! Ah brother! How do you expect me, your younger brother, who is just striving to stand on his feet to carry all these loads alone?

Nwadinobi: Hei! Look!! I‟m not here to banter words with you. It is either you accept my conditions or you forget all about my companionship.

Ugwumba: Hmm! Brother, I must apprise you that you are press-ganging me into accepting your conditions. I‟m accepting your painstaking conditions in the light that, I don‟t want you to say that I snubbed you by asking willing outsiders to accompany me to Onitsha without strings attached.

Nwadinobi: Ehn! I‟m happy that you know our custom at the tip of your fingers. Hei! Youngman! Make sure you don‟t tell me cock and bull stories tomorrow. My Basic Traveling Allowance alias BTA is not negotiable o.

Ugwumba: Don"t worry brother. *Chiokike* will provide your BTA, let me go and see Nnanyi, I learnt, his waist pain has started again.

Nwadinobi: Where is he?

Ugwumba: I was told that he is at the *Obu* by the fireside.

Nwadinobi: [being unconcerned.] Tell him to take heart. I"m on my way to Rumumasi, my in-law"s place. I will be back later in the day. See you then.

Ugwumba: Brother! Are you saying that you can"t spare just one minute to see papa, who is reeling in waist pain as a result of his encounter with you some years back?

Nwadinobi: Hei! Small boy! Don"t let my wrath rouse against you now. Just go and deliver my message to him and stop asking foolish questions. I"m on my way to Rumumasi; if you like you can withhold the message. I don"t give a damn.

The Next Day

Ugwumba: [after the Onitsha trip.] Nnanyi, we came back with the sewing machine, but not without the usual stress from your „first son". He exploited me to the marrow. I spent more than anticipated as a result of his greed.

Dikeoha: My son, do not worry. *Chiokike* will see you through. I"m blissful that you came back with a blessed machine. God will multiply the fruits of your labour hundred fold. Watch out, within a few months you will raise enough shekels to take a wife for yourself. You are blessed henceforth.

Ugwumba: [showing obeisance to his father.] Thank you Nnanyi for blessing me. God will elongate your life.

Dikeoha: Ugwumba! Ugwumba!! Ugwumba!!!

Ugwumba: Nnanyi, I"m listening.

Dikeoha: My son, how many times did I call you?

Ugwumba: Nnanyi, you called thrice.

Dikeoha: You see, the only thing you can do to soothe my heart is for you to get married, a few months after opening your shop for business, I have blessed you, the money for the marriage ceremony won"t be a problem. Hmm! I want to give your wife and you some portions of land and palm trees before I pass on. My days are numbered. Please, keep this to yourself.

Ugwumba: Nnanyi, I will do exactly what you said but *Chiokike* will not allow you to die and leave us at this critical time, when we need you most; if not for anything else, your encouragement and sagacious counsel.

Dikeoha: Ugwumba, my son, I can see and feel your concern for a dying father. Mm! Well, such is life. There is time for everything: time to be born, grow, live and die. You are even lucky to have me around for all these years as a father. I never sense or grope the affection of parents. I lost my parents at a very tender age. Mmm! My son, it will be wise, and for your own good, for you to start consoling yourself right from now, for you may not see my face again in a few months to come. You see, I"m revealing this to you because you are my last son and the only one close to me at home.

Ugwumba: [feeling sad and tearful.] Nnanyi, wherever you may be in time to come, *Chiokike* will safeguard you in His bosom. I hope you will also oversee our wellbeing? However, I will keep this revelation secret as you demanded. Nnanyi, let me go and see Okonkwo and thank him for raising the loan for me.

Dikeoha: My son, it is a wise thing to do. You see, every great wrestler deserves a pat on the back. Extend my appreciation to him.

Ugwumba: Okay, Nnanyi, I will deliver your message to him. Be well.

Scene 13

Obidike: Em, Nwadinobi, where were you coming from in the afternoon with your brother, Ugwumba?

Nwadinobi: Oh! Oh!! So you have not heard? Okay! I went to Onitsha with my brother to purchase a sewing machine and other items for his fashion business. Things are very, very expensive these days o. I spent virtually all my income for the last six months, just to make sure that my brother settles down for serious business.

Obidike: Are you saying that you used your own shekels to purchase the machine, pressing iron and other items for your brother?

Nwadinobi: Yes o. I"m proud that I was able to sponsor the trip and bought those items for my younger brother. At least, I have settled him; he can now plan for his future on a sound footing.

Obidike: Nwadinobi! Your story is hard to chew.

Nwadinobi: What do you mean by that?

Obidike: Look! You are my younger brother and everybody in this village knows what you can do.

Nwadinobi: What does that mean? What are you insinuating?

Obidike: Hei! Listen, if any other person is afraid to tell you the bitter truth, I, Obidike cannot fear you. When will you change from your evil activities? Everyone in this community is aware of your demands on your brother, Ugwumba before you agreed to accompany him to Onitsha. We are also aware, how Mazi Okonkwo raised some soft loans for him. As you can see, vividly, your nakedness has been exposed in the (full) glare of publicity. Why not strive to change for the better before it"s too late?

Nwadinobi: Enough of your vituperation! Yes! It is people like you that thrive in the business of inculcating bad blood in a united family. What is your interest with our family affairs? Is Ugwumba your brother?

Obidike: Ugh! Listen attentively. Ugwumba is a bonafide kinsman and by extension my younger brother. Ugwumba is a young man endowed with humility; he pays tribute to his umunna, especially the elderly as our custom demands. As you can see, whatever that troubles him, affects the entire umunna. *Igwe bu ike* (group is strength). If I may ask, was it not in our presence that you sent him and Uzoma packing with empty hands, after serving you for years? Was it not also before our very eyes that you aborted his marriage to Akueze and later impregnated Mgbafor? Nwadinobi, puah! You don"t have shame in your face. Is it a curse that you must thrive in evil? We all know your criminal records right from childhood.

Nwadinobi: [being so furious.] Look! Obidike or what do you call yourself? I have warned you, enough is enough. Why this trash? If this wagging tongue of yours persists, I will be forced to descend on you.

Obidike: Ugh! You are a mere rat. So you have forgotten my wrestling records as the champion of all the fourteen contiguous villages in Rumubowo, the enlarged clan? A warrior never says die until the end of time. Hei! Let me tell you the truth which I will always tell you at any time and anywhere. You see, when an *arusi* (fetish god) tends to overstep its bounds, the worshipper is impelled to remind her of the sort of wood she is made of. Nwadinobi, you have done enough harm. Reflect on what you have done to your ageing parents. Mm! if, perhaps, nothing is done fast, Nnanyi Dikeoha may die of the waist injury inflicted on him by you. Why can‟t you have pity on your parents? When will you transform for the better? Tufiakwa! What a spell?

Nwadinobi: [realizing that Obidike is a veteran wrestler and that he cannot challenge him to a fight, decided to desert the scene.] Hei! Foolish old man, why can‟t you go home and take care of your household instead of wasting your time here, pokenosing in other people‟s affairs? I‟m leaving you here alone, *añu ofia* (bush meat). You can continue talking to the marine. Puah! *Onye asiri* (a gossip).

Obidike: Look at you! Shameless idiot! Badger! Don‟t you know that you are a bastard? Do you think that you are a product of Dikeoha‟s loin? We know all these things, is it because we decided to be mute? You are a mere butterfly that calls itself a bird; you will perish in shame, useless bastard. You can go to hell and die.

Scene 14

Ugwumba: [three months after the establishment of his workshop.] Nnanyi, now that your prophecy has come true, I wish to announce to you that I have found a damsel whom I would cherish to marry.

Dikeoha: Ehn! Your gist soothes my heart. But where is she from and from which family?

Ugwumba: She is from Rumuezeanyaku near Rumumasi. She is the daughter of Dikeocha, the great palm oil dealer.

Dikeoha: Okay! I know Dikeocha very well. We were childhood friends, but what I do not appreciate is the village, Rumumasi. My dislike is associated with the character of Nwadinobi‟s wife and her family members.

Ugwumba: Nnanyi, as much as Rumuezeanyaku is adjacent to Rumumasi, they are not the same. And moreso, you cannot use the trait of one family to judge another. My fiancée is very down-to-earth. I hope we shall commence marital rituals on her, come next *afor* market day.

Ekechi: [who had been bedridden for a long time, consequent upon the heart attack she suffered as a result of Nwadinobi"s activities, came in.] Nnanyi, I greet you. I overheard what you were saying, so I decided to force myself to this place.

Dikeoha: Hmm! Since you said you overheard us, do you know anything about Dikeocha"s off-springs?

Ekechi: Nnanyi, you know, Dikeocha is an *Ógaranya* (a wealthy man), for he had so many wives and children. Ugwumba, my son, if I may ask, which of the children are you talking about and who is her mother?

Ugwumba: Mother! Her name is Ugoeze (the king's eagle), the daughter of Ochenahu, Dikeocha"s second wife.

Ekechi: Oh! My son, you made a very good choice. The maiden is very humble. I used to see her in the market, assisting her mother.

Dikeoha: Ugwumba! You have to hasten your arrangement; we shall be going there on the next *afor* market day, as you proposed. Meanwhile, you have to go to Rumuezeanyaku tomorrow with your friends for the usual acquaintanceship with the would-be bride"s family.

Ugwumba: Nnanyi, I have already planned to do that tomorrow. Let me go and remind my friends, especially Uzoma, about our journey to Rumuezeanyaku tomorrow.

Dikeoha: Em… no matter how the fire rages in the forest, the Chameleon will always walk slowly in dignity like his ancestors. Go well, my son. I will be very happy to see that this marital ceremony comes to pass, after the sacrilegious deeds of Nwadinobi.

Ugwumba: Nnanyi, you should not bother yourself about Nwadinobi and his activities. *Chiokike* shall see us through in this and other ventures. I will see you people later in the evening.

Ekechi: [as Ugwumba was dashing out.] Hei! Son! Be careful. May our guardian angel guide and protect you.

Scene 15

Ufere Toti: [three months after Ugwumba"s marriage ceremony, Dikeoha gave up the ghost. Subsequently the town crier was mandated by *Ndichie* to announce the death.] Gwom! Gwom!! Gwom!! Eeh! Eeh!! Eeh!! Ewuoh! Chei! People of Rumuoma! I know, you are all in slumber, for this is an unholy hour. Ugh! I wish to inform you all that something mysterious and more powerful than *Nte*, met *Nte* in her trench. Hmm! Hmm!! Hmmm!!! Chei! *Ókeósisi adaalá, Ójii adaalá* (a male tree has fallen, an Iroko tree has fallen). What have we done to deserve this great loss? Death! Why did you extend your cold hand to our illustrious son? Why is it that only the best amongst us are being taken away? Chei! Dikeoha, *Nwoke Obioma, Ekwueme, Ebubedike, Nwannedinamba, agbawuodike isu, dibia mgborogwu, onye udo*, is no more. Ewuoh! *Obodo anyi n' amajijiji, Ókeósisi amajiele, umu nnunu efeliele* (our community is shaking, the male tree has fallen and the birds have flown away). My people, I hope the message is understood? My flute has also delivered the message to our ancestors. Gwom! Gwom!! Gwom!!! Ufere Toti is going; he has delivered the message from Ndichie.

Ezeudo: [in the morning after the announcement of the demise of Dikeoha, led other elders to the bereaved family to commiserate with them and also arrange for the burial rites.] Hmmm!!! Who is here? Ezeudo and Ndichie greet you all.

Ugwumba: [came out to receive Ndichie.] Nnanyi Ezeudo, Ndichie, you are welcome.

Ndichie: Thank you, our son. Where is your mother and other members of your family?

Ugwumba: My mother is beside the bedside of her deceased husband, weeping. Nwadinobi left this morning for an unknown destination.

Ezeudo: Ndichie, let"s go inside and console Ekechi.

Ugwumba: Nnanyi, I will appreciate anything that would soothe my mother from her present bitter state of mind. I don"t want to lose her too.

Ezeudo: [leading other elders to Ekechi.] Ekechi, please take it easy, we appreciate and empathize with you, but you cannot continue this way. There is still life ahead of you. You cannot kill yourself because of the demise of your hubby. Why not allow *Chiokike*, who gives and takes, to handle every situation. We are just mortals, our powers are very limited, we cannot change what *Chiokike* had designed and destined to happen. Please, wipe your tears and clean up because you have a lot of people to attend to. (All left the deathbed).

Ekechi: [tearfully.] Nnanyi, thank you for the words of encouragement. I"m happy to have people like you, as my husband"s Umunna. Em, with people like you around, I know my husband may seem to be dead, but he is not dead.

Ezeudo: Ekechi! Enough of your weeping, you should take solace in the fact that your husband lived a good life. He was one of the respectable men in this community. He left behind indelible footprints. Hmm! Em! In the interim, Umunna had decided to send for Kawawa, since Nwadinobi had become illusive.

Kawawa: [as they were still talking, came in.] Mama! Ndichie! I greet you all.

Ndichie: Thank you, our son. You are welcome.

Ezeudo: Hmm! Chei! Our ancestors are right. It is said that whenever someone"s name is being mentioned and he does not appear physically, it then indicates that he may be caged or dead. My son, Kawawa, did you receive any message to come home?

Kawawa: No, Nnanyi, I did not receive any message. Em, I had a chilly shock, after seeing my father in a vision, so, I decided to come over to see him and mama.

Ezeudo: You have done well, my son. It is true that *Nchi* (the grass-cutter) does not abandon its track, unless she observes a foot print. Hmm! Chei! The day is growing dark, and the birds are returning to their solemn nest, singing dirge.

Kawawa: Nnanyi, I saw some people at the *Obu*, what are you celebrating? Where is my father? Why are you phlegmatic?

Ezeudo: My son, go inside your hut and refresh, this is not the right time to ask questions.

Kawawa: [beginning to sense that all was not well.] Nnanyi, I will not leave this place until I receive answers to my questions. Where is my father? Mama, why are you weeping? Where is Ugwumba and others?

Ezeudo: [cleared his throat.] Hmm! My son, it is hard to chew. You see, we were deliberating on how to send a message across to you before your coincidental arrival. Kawawa! My son, we have lost a gem, the Iroko tree has fallen, and the birds are seeking for a new fortress.

Kawawa: Nnanyi, are you saying that my father has passed on?

Ezeudo: Mm! my son, it is not our tradition to say that, a colossus like your father is dead. Your father, as it were, is not dead. He is on a transition, a pleasurable journey to the other side of the world.

Kawawa: Nnanyi, where lays his remains?

Ezeudo: [led Kawawa and other elders to the deathbed of Dikeoha.] This is the remains of your father, please, take heart and listen to us on the next line of action.

Kawawa: Ewuoh! Chei! *Chiokike*, so my adorable father is no more? Who will be my adviser and backbone? Death! Why are you so cruel? Why should you arrest and cage my beloved father? So, my mentor and fortress have been conquered? Mmmmmh!

Ezeudo: Kai! My son, don"t let your mother see you lamenting o. You should go and encourage her to take heart. We have tried our best to calm her down. You see, what she needs most at this moment is your support and assurance that there is still abundant life ahead.

Kawawa: Nnanyi, thanks for your sagacity and support. Em, I will see you all in a few hours time for the funeral arrangements. Before then, I would have seen and conferred with my brothers.

Ezeudo: You have spoken well, my son. We shall be leaving, until when you send for us, stay blessed. Goodbye.

Kawawa: Nnanyi, Ndichie, *Chiokike* be with you all. Goodbye.

Scene 16

Dikeoha's funeral rites

Dikeoha was given the burial of those that took the traditional title of *Ogbuefi*. Festivities continued for two *orie* market days. During the traditional wakes keeping and burial proper, there was an avalanche of show-off, especially by those who took the *Ogbuefi* title. They paid their last tribute to Dikeoha by excessive brandishing and clanging of matchets, accompanied by war songs and dances. There was also excessive destruction of goods and properties, mainly plants like Banana, Plantain, Palm fruits and pawpaw. All the enlarged clan and people from far and wide were at Dikeoha"s funeral, for they saw him as a great man, who came to serve humanity. Cannons and Dane guns were ceaselessly fired, the esoteric historical drums of death, beat frequently. The *Iko* (wooden) instrumentalists and *Ogbu Opi* (the flutist) performed on top of the roof of Dikeoha"s house. Able-bodied men zoomed about frenetically, destroying every tree and animal on sight, jumping over walls and dancing on the roof. Dikeoha"s age grade members brandished and clanged their *Akparaja* (special ancient war matchets) increasingly with heroic songs and unique skipping dance style. While Dikeoha was lying-in-state, various groups, through their spokespersons delivered orations, sending messages via the deceased to their progenitors in the spirit world. When it was the turn of the people of Rumuoma to deliver their own message, Ezeudo took the stage and opined as follows: ***Dikeoha!*** *You were a great man. Had it been you weren't great in your lifetime, Umunna would have required you to come again with greatness. Hmmm! Dikeoha, had it been you were a pauper, Umunna would have expected you to come again with opulence. But you were a Croesus. If you had been a nincompoop, Umunna would have given you walking papers to come again with sagacity. But you were a sage. Dikeoha! Had it been you were timid in your lifetime, Umunna would have asked you to return with prowess. But you were prodigious. If you had been a sidekick, Umunna would have given you marching orders to return as a pathfinder. But you were a humdinger. Dikeoha! Dikeoha!! Dikeoha!!! The lion with the human heart, your Umunna, is asking you to come again with a heart of equilibrium. Yes! We believed that, had it been that you did not accept Nwadinobi as your son, you would still be revelling in the euphoria of life with us now on this plane. Hmm! Ugh! Your Umunna are lamenting. The womenfolk and children are weeping. Throngs of mourners are beckoning on you to depart in peace if your demise is pristine, but if propelled by unnatural causes, do not allow such a moment's rest.* As Dikeoha was being lowered and the tomb enclosing, mourners and others present began spontaneous wailing, as men and women shout and enumerate the attributes of the deceased, and beckon on the progenitors to receive him well, and allow him to come back and continue with his good work here on earth.

Scene 17

Kawawa: [two days after the internment of Dikeoha, talking with Ezeudo.] Nnanyi, I wish to thank you on behalf of Dikeoha‟s family for your assiduous effort during the burial rites of our dear father.

Ezeudo: Hmm! My son! I did what I ought to do and as such, I‟m not expecting any commendation from anyone. Dikeoha is my right-hand man. Had it been that, he was in my shoes, he would have done the same to me. However, I appreciate your humility and understanding throughout the hectic period of the burial activities. Your father was a great man. I‟m glad he had someone like you and Ugwumba behind. His foot prints are indelible.

Kawawa: Nnanyi, I appreciate your eulogy of my father. Ehn! If I may ask, why did the titleholders, age groups and youngsters destroy my father‟s properties, especially the plants and economic trees.

Ezeudo: Oh! Kawawa, my dear, the action was an indication that your father, Dikeoha, was indeed a hero; and that he should continue to be brave and face all barriers on the way as he journeys to the other side of life. He should be able to destroy evil, the way the various groups destroyed his properties.

Kawawa: Nnanyi, thank you for the explanation. *Chiokike* is wonderful and merciful by keeping Ndichie alive to direct the youngsters towards the right path. Without Ndichie being around, *ngwere* (lizard) would have been delicacies for the youngsters.

Ezeudo: You are right my son, you see, the ceiling won‟t stay when the room is no longer there. Hmm! In the interim, since you seemed to be the real light of the family, I would admonish you to gather all the members of your immediate family and take inventory of the past weeks‟ activities, with a view of putting things back in place. As you know, in an event of this magnitude, many things might have gone out of place unnoticed. Em! Ehn! My son, in whatever you do, please don‟t give Nwadinobi, a scintilla of an impression, to see you as playing the role of the heir apparent, which he claims to be, for he is dangerous.

Kawawa: Nnanyi, are you trying to tell me that Nwadinobi is not the *Opara* (first son).

Ezeudo: Ah! My son, you got it all wrong. It is not the duty of an elder to cause a row amongst brothers. Did your father tell you anything contrary to your belief and view about Nwadinobi?

Kawawa: No, Nnanyi, but he sometimes indicates, proverbially, that Nwadinobi did not take after him like Ugwumba and I.

Ezeudo: My son, your father"s wish has to be respected. He accepted Nwadinobi as his first son and that is the stand of Ndichie. My sincere advice is that you should be chary of him. Aha! Please, my son, wherever you may be after here, makes sure you send messages to your mother and provide for her too. You are no more an infant. Hmm! I have to leave now. I"m expecting some strangers at home. Goodbye.

Kawawa: Nnanyi, your advice is well noted. Meanwhile, I will be traveling back to Lagos with my family members tomorrow, after today"s discussion with members of my immediate family. Goodbye.

Ezeudo: Okay, I will see you by tomorrow in the morning hours before your journey. Goodbye once more.

PHASE FOUR

The Hydra

Some „few" days after the funeral rites of Dikeoha, Kawawa, who was the live-wire of the household, went back to his base in Lagos. Soon after his departure, Nwadinobi began his beastly activities geared towards eliminating Ugwumba and his wife, after diabolically killing their only son, Dede. As a result of the above threat, Ugwumba took his wife and migrated from Nigeria to the Republic of Ivory Coast, through bush tracks and local boats.

Subsequently, Nwadinobi became the only male child at home in total control of all the family properties. He reinvigorated his contact with the Old Nick in order to prevent his younger brothers from remembering home, let alone visiting the same. He wished them death in foreign lands, so that he alone will get hold of all the family belongings, especially lands.

Nwadinobi dealt with a great deal of people through his familiar spirits" activities. He attacked esoterically the legs of his second cousin and the wife. Consequently, they were bedridden for a long time. Fortunately, they belong to the same Umunna. Subsequently, purification rituals were carried out by their maternal parents, as tradition would demand.

The real trouble started when Ugwumba gathered some shekels and came home to build a house on one of the lands given to him by the father, Dikeoha. Nwadinobi refused to allow him to erect the building. He started fermenting trouble deliberately, so that Ugwumba would waste his money on unnecessary litigation. He even fought him physically.

But Ugwumba was not deterred, he went ahead to erect the building. At one stage, he left for Ivory Coast to reinforce more capital for the project. The instant he left, Nwadinobi with the assistance of his son, Osama pulled down the building. This incident occurred three consecutive times. Pathetically, the majority of the Umunna were afraid of him, hence his activities with the devil.

The fangs from Nwadinobi"s claws did not spare his aged mother. Each time Kawawa sends money and other items to Ekechi, for her upkeep, Nwadinobi would do away with the shekels, but if the woman ties the money in her wrapper, he would beat her up and forcefully collect the money from her. However, as this misdemeanour became unbearable, Kawawa, his soldier brother, got in contact with the local divisional police officer, who later invited Nwadinobi to the station and berated him for maltreating his widowed-mother.

It was at this juncture that Nwadinobi intensified his diabolical activities against Kawawa and wished him death at all cost. As a result of chronic mental torture and emotional depressions as propelled by Nwadinobi, his mother, Ekechi died of heart attack and she was buried. Life continued.

After a while Kawawa retired from service, when his children were already in high school. Nwadinobi did not send any of his children to school. It was later in life that the extended family spirit aided some of them to acquire some level of education. One of them called Azika eventually became a serpent in the cloak of a catholic reverend sisterhood, inspiring evil and secularity.

As the civil war broke out, the retired soldier, Kawawa was called to duty by the Biafran side. Unfortunately, he did not return home at the end of the war. Verily, a gem was lost by Dikeoha"s household.

Shamelessly, Nwadinobi proclaimed that it was his oracle that took the life of his own 'brother', Kawawa in the battle field. In consonance with the archaic fetish tradition, Nwadinobi took possession of Kawawa"s prized properties. He went into merriment with his acolytes. At least, he had succeeded in eliminating one of the two, as it were, in his foolish thought!

Subsequent upon Kawawa"s passage, Nwadinobi focused on the elimination and total cleansing of the remaining one, Ugwumba and his household. He started by demolishing Ugwumba"s house, after completion and installation of all necessary facilities. How? One would like to query.

There stood a particular palm tree in front of the new building which Nwadinobi refused to be uprooted during the clearing of the site. He cunningly claimed that he was about to commence tapping on it. Peace was allowed to reign by Ugwumba who looked the other side and continued with his building project.

After completion of the building, it was decided that the palm tree should be uprooted and that the expertise of professionals ought to be employed for the job because of the delicate nature of the situation.

As if specially ordained to perpetuate evil, Nwadinobi bulldozed himself to the centre stage, insisting that he cannot be alive to see „outsiders" collect the wages for a job he can do perfectly.

However, all present knew him very well and as such prevailed on him to dash the thought of carrying out the delicate assignment. Esoterically, before one could spell „masai" Nwadinobi was already on top of the palm tree with his sharp cutlass. He directed the trunk of the palm tree towards the new building, despite public outcry, he allowed the tree to descend on the house, thus demolishing it.

Act Four

Scene 1

Nwadinobi: [three months after the burial of Dikeoha, soliloquizing.] Ehn! Now that the only hindrance to my bid to possess the family"s lands and other properties is no more, I will make sure that, come hell or high water, Kawawa and Ugwumba are sent on exile, never to remember or return home again. Hmm! Who will assist me to achieve my heart's desire? Em! Em!! Yes! Egwuonwu, the *dibia-afa* (a witchdoctor) will definitely have answers to my problems.

Egwuonwu: [in his shrine, rehearsing with his gods.] Mm! Utaka! We have seen a new day. This is kola nut and wine. As the door opens, the mouth follows suit. Utaka, I know that you will receive more clients today. I can see the appearance of the rainbow in the sky. Em!

Nwadinobi: [came around the shrine as Egwuonwu was still busy rehearsing with the idols.] Egwuonwu! Egwuonwu!!

Egwuonwu: Oh heck! Who are you? You can come in.

Nwadinobi: *Dibia-afa*, I greet you.

Egwuonwu: What a manner of greeting? Oh heck! You have come to ask me to send your brothers into exile.

Nwadinobi: How did you get to know about it?

Eguwonwu: Utaka, the spirit, disclosed your mission to me. But, if I may enquire, why do you want to send them far away from home?

Nwadinobi: Em! I want them to die in foreign lands, so that all the landed properties of our father will be mine alone. Egwuonwu! I know you have the magic wand to see the manifestation of my heart's desire.

Egwuonwu: Hei! What did you say your name is?

Nwadinobi: Ah! Egwuonwu! Don't you know me again? I'm Nwadinobi, the first son of Dikeoha.

Egwuonwu: Listen! Dikeoha was a good man and I cannot do any harm to any of his off-springs. It is true that I'm a witch doctor but not the evil type. Utaka, the spirit, is a defender of the oppressed. Ugh! Look! You have to leave this shrine immediately before Utaka reacts against you. Why are you so cruel and greedy? Is it a curse? Who did this to you? I say! Leave now! You bastard!

Nwadinobi: [as he dashed out of the shrine, decided to go straight to his former evil *dibia-afa*, called Okaome.] Okaome! Okaome!!

Okaome: Yes! Who is calling? Please come in.

Nwadinobi: Okaome! I greet you.

Okaome: Hmm, I can perceive your mission. However, you have to drop the usual requirement of *agbala-ogbunabali* (the spirit that kills at night).

Nwadinobi: [deposited some shekels in front of the shrine.] Okaome, I have performed the ritual and all that is expected of me. Ehn! Now, what"s my mission here?

Okaome: Aha!!! Ogbunabali revealed to me that, you have come to solicit my help in order to send your brothers into exile, so that you can inherit all the landed properties of your father.

Nwadionbi: Oh great! Ogbunabali is right.

Okaome: Em! You see, this is a great task since your brother, Ugwumba is still at home, it can not work. You have to frustrate him, so that he can desert home and reside somewhere else.

Nwadinobi: Okaome! I will make sure that he becomes restless and suffers privation. These will definitely force him to abandon home for greener pastures elsewhere. Drat it! Mm! I have to leave now. Goodbye.

Okaome: Goodbye! Greet your wife for me.

Scene 2

Six months later

Ugwumba: [as a result of frustration and intimidation from Nwadinobi, decided to sojourn in Ivory Coast.] Mama! Please take heart, be very careful, so that Nwadinobi will not send you to an early grave. Now, that I"m leaving you behind for Ivory Coast, I know, he will intensify his already cruelty against you. I pray, *Chiokike* will protect you from his fangs. Oh! The vehicle that will convey me to the border is around. I will be sending messages to you from time to time. Please, keep fit and remain blessed. Goodbye.

Ekechi: Have a safe journey, my son. *Chiokike* will wipe your tears; your tormentors will be put to shame, for they will live to see the goodness of *Chiokike* in your life. Your father"s spirit will accompany you throughout your sojourn in the foreign land. Goodbye

Scene 3

Nwadinobi: [after Ugwumba"s departure to Ivory Coast, Nwadinobi went to inform his witch doctor.] Okaome! Okaome!!

Okaome: O yes! Who is that? Come in.

Nwadinobi: Okaome! I greet you and *Ogbunabali*.

Okaome: You are welcome, *Ogbunabali* greets you too. Em, I can see that your brother has gone to sojourn in a foreign land. It is now time to get down to real business. You know, your brother, Ugwumba has a very strong *chi* (guardian angel) as his citadel.

Nwadinobi: Okaome! Okaome!! Listen! Whatever it will take to tame his „chi", I will do more. My mission is clear, that is to make sure, they die in foreign lands. I hope the message is still clear?

Okaome: Nwadinobi, I can see that you are really prepared for this course. *Ogbunabali* will not disappoint you. Ehn! The items for this mission are as follows: two agama lizards, two cocks, two he-goats, two praying mantis, two vultures and their eggs, two empty baskets and two kola nuts and alligator pepper. Em! If you can"t find these items easily, you can give me the shekels to get them for you.

Nwadinobi: Okaome! I have no time to waste, this is the money. You can keep the change.

Okaome: Aha! You have to leave now and return in the night, when the sacrifice will be carried out. At midnight, you will be required to take the sacrifice to Aham River and discharge the same therein. More importantly, make sure that no human being sees you or else the sacrifice will lose its efficacy.

Nwadinobi: Okaome! You have spoken well. I will see you as agreed. Good day.

Okaome: Hei! *Ogbunabali* will be expecting you at midnight o.

Nwadinobi: No skin pain, I will be here.

Okaome: Okay o. Goodbye.

At Midnight

Nwadinobi: [returned at midnight.] Okaome! I greet you and *Ogbunabali*.

Okaome: You are welcome. *Ogbunabali* greets you too.

Nwadinobi: Thank you very much. Please, let"s go straight to the business of the day.

Okaome: [after pouring libation to Ogbunabali, prepared the sacrifice and called Nwadinobi.] Nwadinobi! Nwadinobi!! Nwadinobi!!! How many times did I call your name?

Nwadinobi: Three times, Okaome.

Okaome: Now, you are going to carry these sacrifices in two baskets, one for Kawawa and the other for Ugwumba. I must warn you once again, do not let anyone see you while carrying the sacrifices to the dreaded Aham River. I hope you are aware of the consequences?

Nwadinobi: Okaome! You should know better that the snake does not fear the night. I"m on my way to the river.

Okaome: Hmm! *Ekpere anyi bu ka ogazie* (Okay o, our supplication is that, may it be well).

Nneji: [saw Nwadinobi carrying the sacrifices on his head, as he was on a hunting spree; began to reflect rhetorically.] Hei! What am I seeing? What is Nwadinobi carrying on his head? Where is he heading to at this awful hour? This man is really a hydra. Hmm! Okay, I will not let him see me, but I have to trail behind him to see things for myself.

Nwadinobi: [got to the Aham River and began to soliloquize.] Oh yeah! I told Okaome that the snake is the mother of the night. Mmh! I have discharged the sacrifices as required by *Ogbunabali*, without any living soul seeing me. I have to rush home instantly.

The Next Day

Nneji: [the following day, discussing with some village elders, trying to tell them what he saw last night while hunting; the news, however, brutted abroad like a raging wildfire.] Ndichie, I saw Nwadinobi with my two eyes wide open. He threw the two baskets he was carrying into the Aham River after mentioning the names of his two brothers in his incantations.

Ndichie: Ugh! We said it! What this green-eyed monster will do to this community is yet to manifest. We have just seen an iceberg. He had succeeded in eliminating Dikeoha, now he wants to eliminate Kawawa and Ugwumba. Chei! The spirit of Dikeoha will not allow this to happen.

Scene 4

Nwadinobi: [meanwhile, as the news was making the rounds, he was bickering in the euphoria of a successful mission before the witchdoctor.] Okaome, the mission was a fait accompli. O yes! No living soul saw me.

Okaome: Nwadinobi! Nwadinobi!! Nwadinobi!!! How many times did I call you?

Nwadinobi: Okaome, you called me thrice.

Okaome: [cleared his throat.] Nwadinobi, *Ogbunabali* said, it is not yet uhuru, only time will vindicate your assertions.

Nwadinobi: [in fury.] What are you saying? Are you doubtful of my claims? Listen! I repeat, nobody saw me.

Okaome: [satirically.] Nwadinobi, please don"t be angry with *Ogbunabali*, you are right, but in the interim, let"s talk about other issues of importance.

Nwadinobi: Oh! Okaome, I have just remembered that some strangers will be coming from Kumirukiki to visit me. In this respect, I beg to leave. Goodbye.

Okaome: Goodbye! See you in times to come for the outcome of the sacrifices. *Ogbunabali* said, you should wait for the future.

Nwadinobi: Aha! Okaome, I would have forgotten, please, give me that charm you prepared against my cousin and his wife. I want to deal with them instantly. How can they prosper before me?

Okaome: O yeah! You are right, this is it. I hope you still remember the rules?

Nwadinobi: Thanks a lot, Okaome. I still remember the rules. Em! I have to rush down now to meet my visitors. Goodbye.

Scene 5

A year after

Ekechi: [tearfully complaining to some elders led by Ezeudo about how Nwadinobi manhandled her and took away the shekels sent for her upkeeps by Kawawa.] Chei! Chei!! Ewuoh, Nnanyi Ezeudo, I"m finished. This green-eyed monster, called Nwadinobi, has been forcefully collecting all the money and other items sent to me by Kawawa. As you can see today, this is one of the series of attacks on me. He will definitely regret the course of his life.

Ezeudo: Ekechi, we are sorry for all these acts of rascality from a supposedly adult. We are witnessing a dance of shame. Mm!! On behalf of the entire Umunna, I will send a telegram to your son, Kawawa, apprising him of the activities of Nwadinobi at home.

Kawawa: [after receiving the telegraphic message from Ezeudo called the local police divisional officer, asking him to stop Nwadinobi from maltreating their mother.] Hello sir! Please, I"m Warrant Officer Kawawa of the West African Frontier Force, Lagos division. I would like you to go to Rumuoma, ask about the family of Dikeoha. When you get there, ask of Nwadinobi, take him to your station and warn him sternly to desist from maltreating our aged mother. Your anticipated cooperation is highly appreciated.

D.P.O: Officer! In the solemn spirit of esprit de corps, your wish will be carried out. Remain blessed.

Kawawa: Oh! Correct!

D.P.O: Sergeant Isigwuzo!

Sgt. Isigwuzo: Sir, here I am.

D.P.O: I'M ordering you to go with Corporal Ala-agboso to Rumuoma, and bring one Nwadinobi Dikeoha here immediately. I hope you get the message right?

Sgt. Isigwuzo: Yes, sir.

D.P.O: Right! Now zoom off.

Sgt. Isigwuzo: [after an hour, came back to the D.P.O and did Obeisance.] Shion sir!

D.P.O: Yes! What is it? It better be important!

Sgt. Isigwuzo: Sir, we found it herculean to bring him here.

D.P.O: Mm! Tell me! Tell me!!

Sgt. Isigwuzo: Sir, he wanted to shun our invitation, so we had to force him down here.

D.P.O: Oh correct! Take him to the dark cell; let the senior inmates discipline him, until he comes to his senses. Do you hear me?

Sgt. Isigwuzo: Yes sir!!

D.P.O: [after six hours, brought Nwadinobi from the cell and warned him not to maltreat Ekechi again.] Hei! What is that your name? Listen and listen well! Your naïve rascality against your own mother is undesirable. This will be the last time this station will hear anything about you in respect of the manhandling of your mother or any other person for that matter. You can go for now. You may be invited again in future, if anything happens to your mother. Sergeant! Show him the way out.

Sergeant: O ya! Hydra! Come over this way. Are you a bastard? Why should you mistreat your widowed-mother? Don"t you know that what she needs now is affection?

Nwadinobi: [on his way home from the police station, soliloquizing.] Hmm! Oh heck! So, Kawawa wants to show me that he has powers. I will deal with him ruthlessly. We shall soon know who amongst us, the male tortoise is. I have to see Okaome immediately.

Scene 6

Ekechi: [in her sick bed, a few months after Nwadinobi"s encounter with the local police, talking with Ezeudo and others who came to empathise with her.] Nnanyi Ezeudo, I don"t think that I"m going to survive this mental torture and emotional depression. The cup of transition has refused to pass me by. My solemned prayer is that *Chiokike* should not allow me to have a child as Nwadinobi in my next coming. Please, take care of Kawawa and Ugwumba. Always advise them as your children, for Nwadinobi has an evil look. He is a night owl and thinks too much, such men are dangerous. Nnanyi! Hmm! don"t take the protection of my children for granted o.

Ezeudo: Ekechi, you are not dying, *Chiokike* will heal you of this ailment. Meanwhile, I would like to remind you that your children are like mine for your husband Dikeoha was my right-hand-man. I will not live to see evil happen to any of Dikeoha"s children.

The Next Day

The Town crier: [announcing the demise of Ekechi.] Gwom! Gwom!! Gwom!!! Ewuoh! People of Rumuoma! Death has visited our community again o. Ekechi has gone to meet her husband, Dikeoha. This message is from Ndichie. Funeral activities commence immediately.

Kawawa: [a week after the interment of Ekechi.] Ugwumba! Ugwumba!!

Ugwumba: Brother, here I am.

Kawawa: Ehn! I wish to inform you that the causal leave of absence granted to me by the military authorities will expire in three days' time, so I will be returning to Lagos tomorrow. Em, if I may ask, when are you returning to Ivory Coast?

Ugwumba: Hmm, brother, I have to put certain things in order before going back to Ivory Coast. However, I hope to make the trip in two weeks.

Kawawa: Well, whenever you decide to go back to your station, endeavour to write to me. I wish you journey mercies in advance.

Ugwumba: Brother! I will precisely do what you asked for. I wish you journey mercies too. Meanwhile, let me rush to see my friend, Uzoma.

Ezeudo: [came in, as Ugwumba was about to leave.] Aha! My children, how are you today?

Kawawa and Ugwumba: We are okay Nnanyi, we greet you. How about your health?

Ezeudo: Hmm! My children, I just believe that *Chiokike* will see me through, even though I"m confronting geriatrics. Yes! There is time for everything. I"m merely waiting for the obvious, when my creator will call me back.

Kawawa and Ugwumba: Nnanyi, we pray for your long life. We cannot afford to lose you. Chiokike will listen to our supplications and elongate your lifespan. Nnanyi, as you know, you are our backbone, since our parents are no more. Please don"t talk about returning to your creator at this time.

Ezeudo: My children, you see, *Chiokike* has been merciful to me. Do you know that out of three hundred members of my age grade, only Ekurume and I are still alive today? Mm! As you people have said, let"s wait for the decision of *Chiokike*.

Kawawa: Nnanyi, I was about to come to see you before you came in. Em, I will be returning to Lagos tomorrow for my leave of absence will expire in three days to come.

Ezeudo: My son, you have done well. Your mother"s burial was well organized. You gave her a heroine's burial rite. Em! Ugwumba, when will you be going back to the Coast?

Ugwumba: Nnanyi, I hope to go back in two weeks…

Ezeudo: I wish both of you journey mercies. *Chiokike* will protect you all, iséé!!! My children! I hope to see you again before my demise.

Kawawa and Ugwumba: Thank you, Nnanyi for your fatherly concern. We hope to see you again whenever we are back in town. *Chiokike* will protect you and give you life in abundance.

Ezeudo: My children stay blessed. I have to leave now because I"m expecting my in-laws from Rumuamanze.

Kawawa and Ugwumba: Nnanyi, we will send some messages across to you in the evening. Be well! Please tread with care.

Ezeudo: Okay my children. I will be expecting the messages. Let it be as said.

Scene 7

Two years later

Ugwumba: [came home to erect a building, but Nwadinobi began to cause trouble, so that he (Ugwumba) will waste the shekels meant for the building project on useless litigations.] Brother Nwadinobi! Em, I brought this palm wine and kola nuts including this cockerel to inform you that I would like to commence a building project on one of the lands, especially that one at *Isiobu*, given to me by our father. You see, as tradition would demand, since our father is no more with us, you as the *Diopara* (first son) represents him. It is on this matrix that I came to proffer our father"s legitimate respect and homage to you.

Nwadinobi: Hmm! Have you ended your sermon?

Ugwumba: I have spoken.

Nwadinobi: [tarried for a while looking morose and trying to comprehend whether this was a rhapsody or real, having relied on the charm prepared for him by Okaome, the witchdoctor, against his brothers.] Em! Em!! Yes! Where do you say you want to erect the building?

Ugwumba: I said, at the land given to me in the presence of all of you by our father at Isiobu.

Nwadinbo: [being an avaricious gourmand, did not want to forgo the gifts from Ugwumba, somehow played cool for that moment.] Ehn! Mm!! You should go! We shall talk more about that later. Meanwhile, thanks for the items so presented.

Ugwumba: Brother! You see, there is nothing to talk about later. I merely came to inform you of my plans. I did not come for you to give me land to erect the building; hence our father had hitherto done that.

Nwadinobi: Hei! Don"t you want me to enjoy the drinks? I said, we shall deliberate on this anathema later.

Ugwumba: Brother! I have just informed you about my plans and I believe that the customary process has been followed. Thanks and goodbye.

Nwadinobi: [soliloquizing.] Chei! Chei!! So the charms and sacrifices prepared by Okaome to make sure that Kawawa and Ugwumba do not remember home are ineffective? How can Ugwumba build a modern house in this community? I will put my foot down to make sure that such doesn"t happen, come hell or high water. Let him erect the building and return to Ivory Coast, I will demolish it. Em! Yes! Let me go and see Okaome the *dibia-afa*, ah! No, on second thought, I have to see him on *afor* day when witch doctors are presumed to be efficacious.

Ugwumba: [three days later, summon Ndichie while the foundation of the building was being dug and presented some bottles of schnapps, kegs of palm wine, kola nuts, alligator pepper and a hefty he-goat before them as tradition would demand.] Ndichie you are welcome.

Ndichie: Thank you, our son.

Ugwumba: [cleared his throat.] Ndichie, I called you all in order to present these items to you and also officially inform you that I am erecting a living house. More importantly, to solicit for your traditional blessing of the foundation.

Obidike: [who took over as the spokesperson of the Umunna after the demise of Ezeudo.] Cha! Cha!! Cha!!! Ndichie kwenu.

Ndichie:Yáa!

Obidike: Kwenu.

Ndichie:Yáa!!

Obidike: Kwezuonu

Ndichie:Yáa!!!

Obidike: Ugwumba, our son, you have done well by recognizing that, East or West, home is the best. He, who respects old age, will be well ripe in age. We thank you for the honour done to us today. Chiokike will take control and protect this building and those that will live in it. Your enemies cannot harm you and your household. We are behind you; go ahead with your project. Your ancestors will not allow evil to befall this project. Yes! Ndichie, I hope, I have spoken your mind?

Ndichie: You have spoken well, Obidike. We should move towards the foundation of the building for libation and prayer to our progenitors with the requisite sacrifices.

Ugwumba: [after the libation and prayer by Ndichie.] Ndichie, I thank you all for honouring this invitation. *Chiokike* will prolong your lives, so that you will continue to guide us your children. I greet you, once again.

Ndichie: Thank you, our son for your humility and respect for elders. *Chiokike* will make you an elder. We shall be going now to attend to other issues at home. God bless you and bye for now.

Ugwumba: Goodbye, Ndichie.

Scene 8

Nwadinobi: [at the shrine of *Agbala-Ogbunabali* on afor market day, questioning Okaome the chief priest cum witch-doctor.] Okaome! What is happening? My brothers have been frequenting home without season, after the sacrifices. Yes! I"m suspecting foul play.

Okaome: Nwadinobi, you see, *agbala-ogbunabali* apprised you that, it was not yet uhuru, that only time will tell if you were right. Instead of you to think rationally and make more inquiries you became irrational and grew annoyed. Can one challenge his *chi* (guardian angel) to a wrestling match? What you are witnessing today is the upshot of your fury.

Nwadinobi: Okaome, please come down to my level. What is really amiss?

Okaome: You see, someone, a hunter to be precise, according to *Ogbunabali* saw you when you were performing the rituals at the Aham River, and subsequently reported the issue to Ndichie as against the rules. Meanwhile, *Ndichie* has been monitoring your movements and activities.

Nwadinobi: Okaome, what can I do to reinvigorate the sacrifice?

Okaome: Hmm! Nwadinobi, it is hard to chew. *Ogbunabali* said that I should inform you to forget anything about sending your siblings into exile, because the rules have been repudiated and as such nothing could be done about it.

Nwadinobi: Ah! What about the building project embarked upon by Ugwumba?

Okaome: *Ogbunabali* told me to inform you to let sleeping dogs lie. You see, no matter what we do here on earth, our progenitors watch over us.

Nwadinobi: Okaome! Why are you talking like this? Are you against my heart"s desire or for it?

Okaome: Oh heck! Listen! *Ogbunabali* revealed to me that he was accosted by your late parents last night, who warned him sternly to desist from tormenting their children, Kawawa and Ugwumba.

Nwadinobi: O yes! I can now visualize your game plan. Ehn! Okaome, so you deliberately duped me of my shekels and other items, pretending to do a charm that will send my brothers into exile? Ugh! Do you think that this is a child"s play? Mm!!! Okay, we shall see, amongst two tortoises which of them is male. I"m going.

Okaome: Hey! Where are you going? Will you vamoose from my sight, you recidivist. What an evil goat? Watch out! *Ogbunabali*, the double-edged spirit will visit you when the time is ripe. Yes! You will be compelled to publicly confess your atrocities, shameless pig.

Nwadinobi: [soliloquizing while on his way home.] Hmm!!! Yes! Now that my relationship with Okaome has gone sour, I have to try and re-establish a link with Okagbue, the chief priest of *Ogbu nwata mgbe ndu di ya uto* (the evil that kills a child at his prime). Em! In the interim, I will send a message across to him tomorrow with some kola nuts and schnapps, through my son, Osama.

Scene 9

Ugwumba: [few days after the erection of the building to lintel level.] Brother Nwadinobi, I came to inform you that I will be returning to my base tomorrow. Please, take these shekels for your kola nuts and the entertainment of your visitors.

Nwadinobi: [feigned happiness.] Thanks a lot. I wish you a safe journey.

Ugwumba: Thanks for your understanding throughout the foundation process of my building. Meanwhile, let me go and inform my chum, Uzoma, about my trip to my base tomorrow. I will see you later in the evening.

Nwadinobi: [after the exit of Ugwumba, began to soliloquize.] Chei! Look at this scallywag o! So, he thinks that I"m happy with him? Hmm! I will use this money to prepare a charm against him, so that he will be unable to make a penny to complete this project. Yes! Ehn, the instant he left for Ivory Coast, I will pull down the structure in the night, when no one will see me.

The Next Day

Ugwumba: [about to zoom off to Ivory Coast.] Brother, I"m going, take care of your family. I will send some money and items to you when I get to my base. Goodbye.

Nwadinobi: [mockingly.] Bye, bye o.

Scene 10

Kawawa retired from military service, after Nwadinobi might have destroyed Ugwumba"s building thrice. Pathetically, as the civil war broke out, Kawawa was called to duty by the Biafran side but never returned. Verily, a gem was lost by Dikeoha"s household. Shamelessly however, Nwadinobi pronounced that it was his oracle, *Amadioha* (god of thunder) that took the life of his brother on the battlefield.

Nwadinobi: Ehn! Ndichie, I summoned all of you here to acquaint you with the fact that, it was my oracle that claimed the life of Kawawa.

Ndichie: Chei! Tufiakwa! What did you just say?
Nwadinobi: I said that it was my oracle that eliminated Kawawa on the battlefield.

Ndichie: Tufiakwa! Are you mad? This is an abomination. How can you claim that someone who died in the battlefield was killed by your fetid-oracle? This is heresy o!

Nwadinobi: I went to Okagbue, the dibia-afa and he consulted with the spirit, who in turn revealed this to him.

Ndichie: What prompted you to go to Okagbue in the first place and why did you go alone? So you have been wishing your brother death?

Nwadinobi: Ah! I did not invite you to come and query me o. I only wanted to inform you that as tradition demands, I would immediately take possession of Kawawa's properties.

Ndichie: Hey! Which tradition demands that? You are on your own o; our hands are not in the glove with you. What a disgusting tradition?

Nwadinobi: Why should I seek the services of a Monkey when I can easily talk to the organ grinder? Who cares about your filthy hands not being in the glove with me?

Ndichie: Chei! Chei!! Aru emee!!! (evil has happened). What sort of heartless beast are you? Are you also going to take over the liabilities of your late brother? Will you cater for his wife and children?

Nwadinobi: Listen! I have finished with you people, why not leave honourably? Meanwhile, I"m using this opportunity to ballyhoo that anyone of you who cares, can come over tomorrow in the evening for the celebration of the victory of my oracle. Yes! Okagbue, the priest of *Ogbu nwata mgbe ndu di ya uto*, will also be present. It will be jollification galore!

Ndichie: [as if they were deserting but were actually leaving.] Tufiakwa!!! This is the mother of all evil. What an impudent remark?

Obidike: We are in trouble in this community o. All his offspring are exhibiting the same evil trait. Now that Kawawa is gone, he will focus on the elimination of Ugwumba.

Ndichie: Chei! The spirit of Dikeoha will not allow any evil to befall Ugwumba.

Three Days Later

Nwadinobi: [after celebrating the so-called victory of his oracle, went to consult with Okagbue.] Em!! Okagbue, now that Kawawa is dead, I would like you to prepare for me a juju that will eliminate Ugwumba and his household.

Okagbue: Nwadinobi! Why do you want to eliminate them? You know, Ugwumba and his family are blessed with strong spirits. I can only suppress their progress.

Nwadinobi: Okagbue! Start immediately to prepare juju for that. You will also prepare an „odieshi" charm that will enable me to live longer than my time.

Okagbue: Hmm, you have to produce one human skull, three he-goats, seven kola nuts, two bottles of palm oil, two tubers of yam, seven cowries, pepper and salt, two heads of tobacco, and gunpowder. Ehn! After the sacrifice, you are expected to renew your pledges and reinvigorate your oath with human life, especially those who are close to you every five years.

Nwadinobi: I have heard you. I will get you the shekels for the procurement of the items so far listed.

Scene 11

In spite of all the trouble by Nwadinobi, Ugwumba was not deterred, he continued with the building project, which he eventually completed. A year after completion, he sent his wife home to put all necessary facilities in place. Unfortunately for her, there stood a tall palm tree directly in front of the new structure.

Ugoeze: Nnanyi (Nwadinobi), I wish to invite Mbazuigwe to come and uproot the palm tree in front of the new building.

Nwadinobi: What are you talking about? Are you saying that you want to invite an outsider to come and receive wages for a job I can carry out with ease? Hey! My people, you can see for yourself the fountain of all shenanigans o.

Nduka: [speaking on behalf of Umunna present.] Em, Nnanyi, you should not bother yourself, we know you are ageing and besides the delicate nature of the situation at hand, requires the expertise of young professionals like Mbazuigwe.

Nwadinobi: Kai! I can smell the conspiratorial aroma of this gathering. O Yes! Your antics can"t work this time around. I would not live to see an outsider collect wages for a job that I can do perfectly within my domain.

Nduka: Nnanyi let us be rational! Even though you claimed to have the capability for doing the job perfectly, what if the employer does not need your services, is it a crime? Everyone here present knows your antecedents very well. It would be wise for you to let sleeping dogs lie.

Nwadinobi: Drat it! You are talking to yourself; will you all get out of this place with your busy body traits? Why can"t you mind your business? Shiftless folks!

Umunna: [the instant Ugoeze zoomed off to Mbazuigwe"s abode. Nwadinobi, esoterically like a lightening catapults himself to the top of the palm tree with his sharp edged cutlass. Despite public outcry, he directed the trunk of the tree towards the new building]. Hey!!! Nnanyi! Come down! Come down!! Come down o!!! Do you want to destroy the new house? What is wrong with you? Who sent you? Is it not in our presence that the owner apprised you to leave the job and she left to call an expert? Why are you facing the trunk towards the building? Aru emee!!!

Ugoeze: [as she was returning with Mbazuigwe, saw Nwadinobi on top of the palm tree, cutting the trunk, so that it would fall on top of the building. She began to wail alongside others but all fell on deaf ears, until the expected happened, the new edifice was destroyed.] Chei! Chei!! Chei!!! Chineke! Nnanyi!! What have we done to deserve this wickedness from you? Who sent you? Ewuoh! Ewuoh!! Ewuoh!!! This man has finished us o. *Chiokike*, what is happening? Umunna, I hope you can bear witness to what transpired? Chei!! There is nothing humanly possible we have not done, just to please this man, all we receive in return is wickedness.

Umunna: Our wife! Please stop lamenting; *Chiokike* knows what is right and He will console you and your husband with enormous strength and wealth to rebuild this house. The evil that men do, will definitely visit them.

Nwadinobi: [came down amidst booing and rushed to his hut.] Hey! Will you give way for me, what are you waiting for, can"t you go back to your shanty homes?

Umunna: What a shameless idiot? Ah! In spite of all the family properties in his possession, he can"t even build a small house of his own. Tufiakwa!

Scene 12

One Year Later

Odikazi: [came in to apprise Nwadinobi and Osama about Azika"s admission into the convent.] Nnanyi, I greet you all.

Nwadinobi and Osama: Īyáa!! You are welcome.

Nwadinobi: [expressed surprise at the sight of Odikazi.] My son, where are you coming from at this time of the day, when you ought to be at your duty-post?

Odikazi: Nnanyi, it is true that *Ewi* (rabbit) as well as *Usu* (bat) are never seen in the broad daylight for the fun of it. It is also said that, *Awo* (toad) found limping in broad daylight is either pursuing its prey or a beast or bird of prey is pursuing her.

Nwadinobi: That"s right my son, but what is it that forced the indefatigable *Nte* (Cricket) out of its trench?

Odikazi: [in a hocus pocus mastery.] Nnanyi, where is Azika?

Nwadinobi: [becoming fretful.] What a hokum! Hey! Listen to me young man; your craftiness can‟t bamboozle me. Now, if you don‟t have any business being here, you better vamoose. What a manner of dilly-dallying?

Odikazi: Nnanyi, don‟t be angry with me. It‟s just that, I‟m overjoyed about Azika‟s feat at the entrance examination which I helped her to enroll for, some months back. She performed creditably well.

Osama: [being curious.] Em! What ilk of exam is that?

Odikazi: Em, it is one of the most pursued exams in vogue today. We are indeed lucky to have one of our own as one of the infinitesimal number of successful candidates.

Osama: [agitating.] Ah! Odikazi! What a cagey craft? Why do you prefer to rigmarole over questions? Since we have been speaking with you, you have not answered any of our questions satisfactorily. Why the tortuous explanation?

Azika: [dashed in as Osama was still talking, and greeted all] Nnanyi, I greet you all.

All: Íyáa! You are welcome.

Odikazi: [having seen Azika, announced the enigmatic anathema.] Ehn! Nnanyi, your daughter, Azika has been offered an admission into the Catholic convent at Rumuokoroshi, where she will join the reverend sisterhood.

Azika: [elatedly.] Oh! This is cheering news? Brother Odikazi, you are indeed a harbinger of good tidings.

Odikazi: Nnanyi, the onus is now on you to see that this journey is followed to its logical conclusion. The education of the girl-child is seminal.

Nwadinobi: [agitating.] Em, I"m not in support of her attending any Whiteman"s school, it is a waste of resources to send the girl-child to school. It is not our tradition. It is abhorred, besides, I"m not well-heeled.

Odikazi: [cut in.] Nnanyi, things have changed. As you can bear witness, most of our people have been sending their female children to school for ages now. The education of the girl-child is a sine qua non for the development of our society. You see, an educated woman breeds good and well-behaved children. Em, the issue of not being well-heeled is unfounded; hence the cost of education is significantly cheap in this realm. Moreover, you are not stint, Nnanyi.

Osama: [cholerically.] Hey! This sermon of yours is only good and comforting to the marines. Papa has said it all, we are not in any position to sponsor Azika to any school. Yes, this is our stand. I hope the message is clear?

Azika: [sobbed out.] Oh! Oh!! So, brother Osama, this is what you and papa are saying? You want to destroy my future and ruin my life, just because I"m a girl. Is it a crime to be a female-child? What a novel world of the male chauvinist pigs? Did I create myself? Is it not *Chiokike* that made me a female?

Odikazi: [while consoling Azika.] Em, please, Azika take it calmly, *Chiokike* will see you through these trying times. Em! Nnanyi, please may I beckon to you once more to reconsider your stand on this issue. Azika is your brilliant daughter and I know she will make you proud in future after her education. Besides, she will be in a position to cater for you at your old age.

Nwadinobi: [absolutely seething.] Ugh! Look! Let her go to blazes with her future assistance, we don"t need it. Em, you can sponsor her education and reap the fruit thereinafter. Yes, for the final time, please take her out of this place and never return here again with the same sour story. You are a bode of bad tidings! What a bogey! What an iconoclast! Jonah!

Odikazi: [while Azika was still grizzling.] Azika! Please let"s leave your father and brother alone for now. Em, I will see what I can do about your education.

Osama: [cut in.] Yes! You have to leave now, to avoid a tauten situation. What the blazes do you think you"re doing? You nosy parker! Let me warn you, this issue is an anathema to us. We will resist any sermon geared towards impelling us into iconoclastic demeanour. I pray, the message is elucidated?

Odikazi: [stoically, as he was deserting the scene with Azika.] Em, Azika, please, don"t bother yourself all that much. I will arrange for your registration formalities this coming week. Look, do not be distracted by your parents" action, they are quite aware of the importance of the girl-child education, it"s just a case of sheer abdication of pristine responsibilities.

Azika: Thank you brother, you are a corker.

Odikazi: Thanks for the accolades.

Azika: You"re welcome, brother.

Odikazi: Em, I want to assure you that, I will put in place an impelling diplomatic stratagem which will make your parents acquiescent in your educational pursuit. Verily! I say unto you, I cannot allow them to weasel out of this all important responsibility.

Azika: Oh, brother, what could I have done without your benevolent spirit?

Odikazi: Never mind! To be noblesse oblige is the spirit and essence of humanity, nothing less.

Azika: Oh!! Brother!!! I will live to cherish this moment throughout the days of my life. You are indeed a good-natured feller.

Odikazi: [pondering.] Cherish! Will you cherish it? Hmm, only if that evil gene that produced you will be concussed, perhaps you may remember this day momentarily, afterall, hibernated squirrels and hedgehogs retain their pristine being. Yes! The viper lives and dies with its venom.

Azika: Ah! Brother Odikazi, you look morose, why the sudden hiatus, anything the matter?

Odikazi: [being snaky.] Em, Azika, there is nothing to worry about. The *Diochi*e (palm wine taper) does not reveal all that he saw while on top of the palm tree. It shall be well; you must accomplish your educational desire, as long as *Chiokike* gives us life.

Azika: Thank you once again, brother.

Odikazi: You"re welcome.

Azika: Em, brother, let me go and inform my friend Adaugo, the daughter of Nnanyi Anunuebe about my admission into the Convent. I will see you later in the day.

Odikazi: That"s right, extend my greetings to her ménage.

Azika: Okay, brother.

PHASE FIVE
The Lamentation

Two years later, Ugwumba returned home and rebuilt the demolished edifice. Unfortunately, some months later, his wife, Ugoeze was attacked by a strange snake in her abode, and the woman died. Consequently, Nwadinobi and his household went into merry-making. The following year, his children, their wives and grandchildren occupied the house, since Ugwumba was still sojourning in Ivory Coast, and they lived therein for over a dozen years, messing up the residence to its foundation before moving to their own house. Soberly, Nwadinobi indulged in the act of impregnating other people"s wives and young girls, thereby producing bastards all over the village. Ugwumba"s first surviving son, disappeared to an unknown land for decades.

God Almighty was so graceful and merciful to Nwadinobi who was over ninety years but resisted all efforts to get him repented from his diabolical activities before his demise. Pathetically his offsprings were exhibiting the traits of their father; even on a higher magnitude, hence a corrupt tree begets corrupt fruits.

Nwadinobi suffered from paralysis, as his limbs withered before his demise. Some of his children and grandchildren died mysteriously and the speculation was that he used them to renew his life oath as ordered by Okagbue, the witchdoctor. He and his first wife who gave up the ghost before him also suffered from paranoia. She, however, confessed some of her evil deeds alongside her hubby before she passed on, despite all efforts by her children to shield her from the public as the confession was flowing out deliberately. Presently, Umunna dreads the family of Nwadinobi with utmost detest. A general sanction or ostracization known as *Ikpikirinkwu* was imposed on them. Nwadinobi was more of an imbecile, who looked morose, mute and excreted freely before his death.

Act Five

Scene 1

Ugwumba: [two years later, returned home from Ivory Coast to rebuild his damaged house.] Chibuike! Chibuike!!

Chibuike: Nnanyi, here I"m.

Ugwumba: Ehn! My son, please go and ask Mazi Okpuzu, the builder, to come over and see me.

Chibuike: Nnanyi do you mean that bricklayer living at Isi Uzo near Ukwu-Ube?

Ugwumba: That"s right, my son.

Chibuike: Okay, Nnanyi, I"m on my way.

Ugwumba: *biko jé ósósó* (Please go quickly)

Chibuike: [came back after a few minutes.] Nnanyi, I have delivered your message, in fact, he is behind me.

Okpuzu: [came in as Chibuike was still talking with his father.] Ah! Nnanyi Ugwumba, when did you return from Ivory Coast?

Ugwumba: Okpuzu, my brother, I returned a few days ago. How about your ménage?

Okpuzu: All is well, Nnanyi. You are welcome. How about your household?

Ugwumba: Em, my ménage was intact when I left for home; I pray it shall remain the same by the time I return to my base.

Okpuzu: Nnanyi, *Chiokike* will protect your ménage. You will return safely to see them in good health. *Chiokike* will give you and your household the heritage of those who fear him.

Ugwumba: Īséé!!! May *Chiokike* harken to your solemn petitions.

Okpuzu: Íséé o. It shall be well with us…

Ugwumba: [cut in.] Chibuike! Chibuike!!
Where is this youngster? Chibuike!!!

Okpuzu: Em,Nnanyi, maybe he is not within. You know these youngsters with their exuberancy.

Ugwumba: [cut in.] You are right my brother. Em! Uwa! Uwa!!

Uwa: Nnanyi, here I come.

Ugwumba: Ehn, my son, please go inside the house and get us some kola nuts, osé óji (Alligator pepper) and a keg of Nkwu-elu (up palm wine.)

Uwa: Okay, Nnanyi, (zoomed off and came back in a jiffy). These are the items, Nnanyi.

Ugwumba: Íyáá! My son, you have done well. Em! May I implore you not to go far from here, hang around for I may require your services soon?

Uwa: Okay, Nnanyi.

Ugwumba: Ehn, my brother, Okpuzu, this is kola nut, as our tradition would demand.

Okpuzu: Nnanyi, I have seen the kola nut, please, may the king"s kola nut remain with him.

Ugwumba: Are you implying that I should bless the kola nut?

Okpuzu: Yes, Nnanyi, since you are my elder.

Ugwumba: Em! With the authority bestowed on me by our tradition as an elder, I"m delegating you to bless the kola nut.

Okpuzu: Thank you Nnanyi for finding me worthy to bless the kola nut, in spite of the age bracket.

Ugwumba: Okpuzu, my brother, you are an amiable, industrious, middle aged bloke. You see, when we realize that age is a case of number and not a measure of personality and sagacity, peace will reign in our society.

Okpuzu: Nnanyi, you have spoken well. Please let"s remove our hats for the supplication.

Ugwumba: That"s right my brother, I"m ready.

Okpuzu: [cleared his throat.] *Chiokike*, we are beckoning you to come and bless this kola nut for us, and also bless my host and his ménage. Grant us procreation, good health, longevity, wealth and good neighbourliness in our time and time to come. Íséé…!

Igwumba: Íséé!!! Ehn, Okpuzu, you have prayed well. You are the son of your father. Uwa! Uwa!!

Uwa: Nnanyi, here I"m.

Ugwumba: Ehn, my son, please break the kola nut and serve us the palm wine as tradition would demand.

Okpuzu: [after the refreshment.] Nnanyi, thanks for the refreshment. Em, it is said in our community that, after such entertainments, the onus is on the stranger to divulge his mission.

Ugwumba: [cut in.] Hei! Point of correction, Okpuzu. You see, as far as I"m concerned, you are not a stranger; you are my kinsman and brother.

Okpuzu: Thank you, Nnanyi for finding me worthy of being your brother. Em, actually, Uwa said you asked me to come over. Please, may I know why my mentor needed my presence?

Ugwumba: Mm! you have spoken well, my brother. You see, since the demolition of my edifice by Nwadinobi, *Chiokike* has been on my side, inspiring me to rebuild the house. It is on this matrix that I repose my trust in you as the man who will do the rebuilding job for me.

Okpuzu: Nnanyi, I empathise with you on the devilish act by your seemingly elder brother. Em, I will not betray your trust in me. I will put in my best to make sure that the house is rebuilt to an acceptable standard.

Ugwumba: Thank you, my brother. Em! When do you think it will be convenient for you to commence work?

Okpuzu: Nnanyi, the onus is on you to say. I"m always at your service. You see, whatever affects you affects the entire Umunna. You are a good man like your parents and brother, Kawawa. Why not allow us to start work on the building tomorrow.

Ugwumba: Okpuzu, thanks for your eulogistic speech. Em, I have no problem with you starting work tomorrow. You can go ahead as suggested.

Okpuzu: Nnanyi, I have to leave now. See you tomorrow bye, bye.

Ugwumba: Good bye, my brother. *Chiokike* will see us through, in our genuine endeavours.

Scene 2

Ugwumba: [addressing his Umunna after the rebuilding of his house and the attendant revelries.] Mm! Umunna, I thank you all for your support and encouragement throughout the demanding stages of this project, may *Chiokike* guard and guide you from the claws of the evil ones in our midst.

Umunna: Íséé!!!

Obidike: [spokesman for the Umunna.] Ugwumba, we appreciate your benevolent spirit towards your Umunna, *Chiokike* will always inspire you and increase the works of your hand. Em, now that you have rebuilt the house, are you going to return home and occupy it or leave it to lay fallow? I know you are aware of Nwadinobi"s activities so far. Mm! my instinct tells me that, if you allow this house to lay fallow, Nwadinobi may occupy it.

Ugwumba: Nnanyi Obidike, I appreciate your brotherly concern. Actually, I do not envisage coming back finally in the near future. More importantly, I don"t want to come home and start struggling for our father"s properties, especially land with Nwadinobi. I need to make some money over there to take care of my children"s education. I don"t wish to be distracted by land-related problems at home at least for the moment.

Obidike: Em! My brother, we appreciate your sagacity. We wish you well, whenever you return to your base in Ivory Coast. We hope you are not leaving immediately?

Ugwumba: Yes, Nnanyi, I have to put one or two things together before my departure.

Obidike: That"s right, your Umunna wishes you well and journey mercies whenever you decide to go back. Em, we have to leave now. Goodbye.

Ugwumba: Thanks to you all, Umunna, I appreciate your hilarity, empathy and support. This shows that the spirit of erima is extant in our community. Adieu.

Scene 3
Three months later

Osama: [talking with his father, Nwadinobi.] Ehn! Papa, em, now that Ugwumba has rebuilt the house, I would like to pack into the house with my family.

Nwadinobi: Ah! You don"t need to tell me. Pack in immediately, after all Mgbafor"s children had occupied some of the rooms. Go in and devastate the building to its foundation. Yes, Ugwumba must be forced out of this environment and the onus is on you to accomplish this listed goal. I hope you have not forgotten whose son you are?

Osama: Ah! Papa, how can I forget? I"m the son of the snake, the queen of darkness, whose offspring are the prince and princess of the night. Can the Vulture beget an eaglet?

Azika: [dashed in as Osama was still talking with his father.] Papa, I greet you all.

Nwadinobi: Thank you, my daughter. How about your academic studies?

Azika: Papa, I"m managing with the little shekels which I do receive from your brother and other members of the extended family.

Nwadinobi: [fretfully.] Hei! Who asked you how you are funded? If you like, you can acquire funds from hell, that"s your own cup of tea, afterall, I didn"t send you to school. Was it not Kawawa"s son, Odikazi and others, who insisted that you must go to school? Em, let them bear the burden. Please, if you want me to be happy with you, don"t repeat that issue again. Ehn, if I may ask, why can"t you get married, so that I can have some change, I mean shekel in my pocket.

Azika: [while sobbing.] Is it what you have to say papa? Ugh! I should get married inorder for you to collect my bride price, while my mates are in school for a better future.

Osama: [barged in.] Which kind of better future? Better future for my foot. What manner of horseshit are you talking about? Papa is right; you should get married and stop reducing our ration in this house. Who told you that female education is approved by our society not to talk of being a Roman Catholic Reverend Sister?

Odikazi: [came around as the discourse was raging.] Nnanyi, I greet you all. You see, I heard all what you have been saying about the education of the girl-child and sisterhood. Em, I wish to inform you that…

Nwadinobi: [cut in.] Hei! You are the cause of this problem. What an anathema? Look! Make sure, you take her out of this place now and never again must you table her case to us, until she gets married. How do you expect a responsible family to waste resources on female education? I hope it is high time you desert from our sight? (Sigh) you nitwit!

Odikazi: [while consoling Azika.] Please! Azika stop the sobbing; let"s leave your father and brother alone for now. I will try my best to ensure that you continue with your education. As you are aware, ignorance is a disease whose only panacea is awareness. I may go back to them later, when their tempers must have subsided.

Azika: [as they entered Kawawa"s parlour.] Brother Odikazi, I appreciate your concern, but don"t you think that returning to my father and brother on this issue may spell doom to you? Yes! They may assault you o.

Odikazi: Em, you are absolutely right. I am aware that your parents are merely avoiding their responsibilities; and any attempt to make them responsive will be stoutly resisted. However, I will diplomatically get them involved in your education no matter the level, afterall; they will be the beneficiaries in the near future. Moreover, an aphorism has it that, if you know the person who will inherit your properties when you die, if you ask him to do something for you and he refuses, continue to ask him, he will definitely listen to you someday.

Azika: Brother! Are you saying that *importuning* does pay off?

Odikazi: Yes, it does pay, no matter when, the end-result is always positive, although unwillingly.

Azika: [cut in.] Ah! Brother, who cares, whether willingly or otherwise, what matters is the end-result. I appreciate your encouragement, I promise to be of help, whenever I"m in the position to do so.

Odikazi: [pondering.] Mm! Look at who will assist another person. Even if she is in a position to do so, the evil gene in her system will prevail, afterall is she not the daughter of an antelope? Is she not embedded in the same attire with her parents? Chei! What an evil gene?

Azika: Ah! Brother Odikazi, you look morose, anything the matter?

Odikazi: Em, there is nothing to bother about, my sister. I was just pondering over your movement back to school tomorrow. You see, Ugwumba sent some shekels to me, which need to be changed into our local currency and this will prompt me to travel to Aba tomorrow.

Azika: Okay! If that is the situation, I have to postpone my trip to school till next tomorrow.

Odikazi: Ehn! That will be better. In the meantime, take this shekel for your shopping tomorrow before my arrival from Aba. Let's forget, I have an appointment with my friend, Onyirimba at Rumuamaoji. Keep fit, until I return, bye, bye.

Azika: Bye, bye, brother.

Scene 4
Eight years later

Visitors: [came to see Nwadinobi in his sick bed.] How are you today, Nnanyi?

Nwadinobi: [while gnashing his teeth in agony.] Oh! Oh!! Oh!!! *My heart is sore pained within me and the terrors of death are fallen upon me.*

Visitors: [pawkily.] Nnanyi, ah! It is not yet time for sore pain and terrors of death to overshadow you. Are you not the indefatigable Nwadinobi, whom, danger and death dread?

Nwadinobi: [in agony.] Hmm!!! My visitors, fearfulness and trembling are come upon me. Horror had overwhelmed me, for the grim reaper is extant.

Visitors: Nnanyi, this sickness of yours is taking a strange dimension o! Is it transforming into paralysis? What might have been the cause of this strange illness? Even your wife, Nmabaraego, had been bedridden for a long time now, and the sudden demise of your children. Nnanyi, something had to be done fast o, so as to avert an impending doom.

Nwadinobi: [after looking morose, uttered.] Do you know about *Nkapi* (a rat-like animal with offensive smells - skunk)?

Visitors: Yes, Nnanyi.

Nwadinobi: You see, the gene that engenders the offensive smells is embedded in *Nkapi.*

Visitors: Em, Nnanyi, are you saying that the cause of your sickness and that of your wife could be traced within your Menage?

Nwadinobi: Hm! My visitors, I have now realized what Okaome told me, when we had a misunderstanding.

Visitors: [curiously.] Nnanyi! What did Okaome tell you?

Nwadinobi: Em!!! He said that at the end of time, my sins will visit me and I will confess….

Osama: [bashed in.] Nnanyi, I greet you all.

Visitors: Íyáá, Osama, how is your mother faring?

Osama: Hm, mama"s health is deteriorating as the day rolls by. She can"t even recognize anything.

Visitors: Oh! So she is suffering from paranoia?

Osama: No, Nnanyi, I think she suffers from concussion and hypnotic trance.

Visitors: Chei! What a double disaster. Em, we shall go and see her immediately.

Osama: It is well Nnanyi; I shall meet you over there in a jiffy.

Visitors: Em, before we miss our way, which of the huts can we find her?

Osama: [pointing to a particular hut.] She is in that big hut, my friend Iteigwe is there too.

Visitors: Okay! You have done well. Please tell Nnanyi Nwadinobi (as he was slumbering) that we have gone to see Nmabaraego, perhaps we may exit from there.

Osama: Okay, Nnanyi, I will deliver your goodwill message. See you later.

Scene 5

Visitors: [at Nmabaraego"s hut.] Mm! Nmabaraego, how are you today?

Nmabaraego: [looking morose as if in a hypnotic trance, managed to utter some incomprehensible words.] I ….am in… g r e a t pain.

Visitors: Nma! We are sorry for your plight and that of your husband. Em, but how did this ailment happen simultaneously with that of your hubby? We meant when did the ailment start?

Nmabaraego: [stressfully.] Em!!! When this sickness started, my son, Osama went to consult with the divinities (oracle) and he was told that I was an accomplice to my husband"s diabolical activities against his brothers and others.

Visitors: Chei! The gods are not to blame o.

Nmabaraego: Em!!! Even my husband was apprised by Okaome a long time ago that he will reap the fruits of his evil seeds. Mm!!! My people, the oracle said that there will be no remedy other than death. Ehn! We eliminated Ugwumba‟s first son, Dede and Kawawa, we also sent Ugwumba‟s surviving first son on exile and conjured the snake that bit his wife.

Osama: [dashed in as his mother was reeling out her misdeeds.] Chei! Mama!!! Stop talking. Em! Please, my people as you can see, she needs some rest, and as such you are advised to leave now.

Nmabaraego: [while coughing.] Em!!! Osama! Leave them alone, I have not finished, I have a lot to say.

Osama: [fretfully.] Hey! Look! I said you should leave now!

Visitors: Okay, we are leaving, but no matter how you conceal the smoke, it must find her way out.

Osama: [cut in.] Hei! What smoke are you talking about? Look! If I hear this nonsense outside, I swear with my gods I will deal with you people mercilessly.

Visitors: [pawkily.] Ah! Please don‟t deal with us o. We are on our way out. As you can see, we only came to sympathize with your ménage on her recent manifesting calamities. Goodbye.

Osama: Ehn! Goodbye, but remember to tell no one anything about my mother‟s talk.

Visitors: [on their way home.] Chei! Chei!! What manner of clone-antelope are we dealing with? Mm! The evil dynasty had been entrenched in our hitherto serene community o…

Ufu: [one of the visitors, cut in.] My people! Did you observe that Nmabaraego was defecating and urinating on her sick bed?

Visitors: Yeah! We saw it all. Ufu, we suspect that the spirits of Dikeoha and Ekechi are tormenting her and Nwadinobi.

Ufu: Yes, your observation is in order. Perhaps her confession is not unconnected with the spirits of Dikeoha"s ancestors.

Visitors: You are right, Ufu. You see, Nwadinobi and his household had committed unfathomable sacrilegious acts.

Ufu: That is true, apart from eliminating some members of his immediate family, he engaged in the act of impregnating our daughters and wives.

Visitors: Ufu, we are finished, indeed we are in real trouble o. You see, when these bastards from Nwadinobi"s loins begin to grow, our community will be transformed into a den of diabolical people and bandits.

Ufu: Chei! What manner of trouble are we confronted with? Mm! It is factual that one bad tree has the propensity of destroying an entire forest, if not checked or felled on time.

Visitors: Kai!!! Can you see how this import from Osueke"s loin into our community is pensively devastating the fabric of our society?

Ufu: [as the visitors get to Ogboto-Ukwu.] Em, my people, *Chiokike* will take charge of our battle. The Old Nick and his agents can"t triumph for long.

Visitors: Ufu! You have spoken very well, you really made our day; may we call it a day at this juncture, goodbye (they all chorused).

Some hours later

Osama: [pondering.] Mm!!! Chei! Now that my mother has lost her memory, prompting her unreflective comments, I have to take her out of the presence of our Umunna and Umundomi.

Mm! Her legs are decaying, day after day with offensive emissions. What a sticking point? Where will I take her for seclusion? Who will be willing to accommodate her? Yes! That"s it. I will hibernate her at my in-law"s abode in Rumuishi. Ehn! The place is a pretty distant hideout.

Scene 6

Two months later

Okengwu: [addressing his Umunna.] Mm! People of Rumuishi, this is not the right time to chop kola nuts as tradition would demand. Em, Okengwu your brother is bereaved.

Umunna:[curiously chorused.] Okengwu! What manner of joke is this? Who is dead? When and how?

Okengwu: Oh! It is hard to chew. What is bigger and stronger than *Nte* visited her in her trench unexpectedly.

Umunna: Look! Okengwu, you have not answered our question o. Stop rigmarolling. Tell us who kicked the bucket. Nothing is strange on the face of the earth.

Okengwu: [breathe a sigh of relief.] Em! My in-law, who was brought here by her children some months ago for medical attention, died last night.

Umunna: Chei! Aru eme!!! What an abomination? So, your mother in-law had been with you in this community without the knowledge of your Umunna. This is against our mores. Okengwu! What is wrong with you?

Okengwu: [curiously.] Em, Umunna, what do you mean by these sayings? I am confused.

Ichie Anosike: [spokesman for the Umunna.] Hey! Youngman, it is an abomination in our community for a man"s in-law to die in his house. Yes! It is an omen of concern.

Okengwu: [still curious.] Nnanyi, what shall we do in order to avert any imminent calamity?

Ichie Anosike: Em, appropriate cleansing will be carried out at your in-law"s abode; for your information the propitiatory sacrifice is very, very tasking and expensive.

Okengwu: [discomposed.] Ugh! Nnanyi, the journey is too far for me o!!! Where will I get the shekels for the sacrifice, after spending all my shekels on my late mother-in-law's ailment?

Ichie Anosike: Drat it! Is it not your ant-infested wood that invited the lizard to the feast? Why didn"t you send your mother-in-law back to her home when it became obvious that she was about to give up the ghost? Afterall, we learnt that she was brought here half-dead.

Okengwu: Nnanyi, actually I made an effort to take her to her abode but her children insisted that she be left here.

Ichie Anosike: [cut in.] Oh heck! Why did the children insist that their mother should remain and die in a foreign land?

Okengwu: Mm! Actually, it is hard to chew, but I have to say it. They revealed that their mother was hypnotically confessing her ménage"s atrocities, and as such she needs to be shaded from the public, especially their Umunna and Umundomi.

Ichie Anosike: Chei! Umunna! Are you here with me?

Umunna: [rambling.] Yes! This revelation tingles the ear. How can one become a recluse or a hermit in the midst of a whole community, if not of evil spirit? Em, we hope and pray that her daughter will not pollute our peaceful community. But the Zebra can"t discard her toga. What an omen?

Ichie Anosike: [cut in.] Young man! What sort of family did you go to take a wife? Did your parents carry out any investigation about the family of your wife before the marriage proper? Ah! You disappointed me, our young men behave and act owlishly.

Okengwu: Nnanyi, actually I met my wife at one of the local schools and one thing led to the other. I later convinced my parents of her good background without digging into her family annals. But my wife is a good person.

Ichie Anosike: Mm! Umunna, it is not our tradition to chuck away the child with the grubby water, neither is it our custom to lament over spilled oil, but it is our duty to clean up the messed ground. Em, we shall dispatch emissaries to Rumuoma to acquaint Okengwu"s in-laws on the demise of their matriarch. Thereafter, we shall embark on the atonement of the sacrilege.

Umunna: Ichie! You have displayed sagacity. Your thought is our thought. May Chiokike see us through this turbulent season o.

Ichie Anosike: Okengwu, I hope you still remember that the sacrifice is very, very expensive and tasking too? At least two big goats are required apart from other items. Em, my people, in the absence of any other issue of urgent attention, I think we should disperse.

Okengwu: Ndi Ichie, Umunna, I thank you all for your support and understanding.

Umunna: [as they were about to leave.] Okengwu! We appreciate your situation right now, but we hope other young men will learn a lesson from your present predicament.

Nwakaibeya: [a member of the Umunna, cuts in.] Yes! Young men should be advised to acquaint themselves very well with their would-be brides, to avoid the contamination of an entire community with the offsprings of *Ekwensu*, the Old Nick. Em, Okengwu, take heart, we are on our way home.

Okengwu: Goodbye, Umunna.

Scene 7

Okengwu: [three days after the propitiatory sacrifice at Rumuoma.] Ehn! Osama, my in-law, now that all the atonement has been accomplished, we have to put our heads together for the burial arrangement.

Osama: Em, you are right my in-law. Actually, members of my ménage have already contacted our daughter, Azika who resides in *Obodo Oyibo* (white man"s country) after her ordination as a reverend sister.

Okengwu: [cut in.] Yes! Tell me, tell me! What did she say? What arrangement is she making? Will she come home for the funeral?

Osama: Hey! Take it easy, bloke. Why such questions? I hope you are also pondering over your own share of the funeral budgets? You can"t pass the buck to anyone.

Okengwu: [miffed.] What sort of funeral budget are you expecting from me after spending all my shekels, taking care of your mother?

Osama: Em, you see, you young men of nowadays, reason with the anus instead of the head. I"m here talking of the present and you are rewinding the hands of the clock backward. Maybe, you don"t even know the type of family you came to take a wife from.

Okengwu: [pondering on his experiences with his in-laws, so far.] Chei! The black widow can never conceal its poison. What manner of family can treat her in-law so badly? Mm! I am finished. It dawned on me now that all my efforts towards the uplifting of this family goes unsung without a modicum of appreciation.

Osama: Ehn, Okengwu, let me be sincere with you, this is not the time to ponder, rather it is time for action. You see, our in-laws are expected to contribute money for the purchase of one big cow, beside drinks, bags of rice, assorted foodstuff. Musicians will also be hired by our in-laws.

Okengwu: [still miffed.] Osama! If I may ask, what will then be your family"s contribution towards the burial rites of your own mother, if we, the in-laws, are expected to carry the entire burden in spite of our hitherto contributions? Don"t you know that we have other responsibilities? Where do you expect us, especially me, to get such shekel?

Osama: [cut in.] Hey! Young man, we are not here to banter words. I don"t give a damn how you get the money, so long as you contribute your own quota of the funeral budget. Let me apprise you that we have our own role to play, for instance, making sure that Kawawa and Ugwumba"s ménage are sidelined. Yes! Azika instructed that some bouncers should be contracted to prevent them from participating in the burial ceremonies. More importantly, they should not be allowed to see the corpse.

Okengwu: [cut in.] But why should an ordained reverend sister dishout such unholy instructions? She is creating an abyss of disunity and hatred amongst members of your extended family, which is against the spirit of Erima.

Osama: Okengwu! Em, you will not understand.

Okengwu: Understand what? Do you want to justify such ungodly instructions? After all, I was meant to understand that Ugwumba"s house harboured all of you including Azika, whom Odikazi and others sponsored in school. What manner of Catholic sisterhood does she belong to?

Osama: Ah! Youngman, why are you indifferent to this noble course? After all, other in-laws have accepted the instructions wholeheartedly and pledge to see to its full implementation.

Okengwu: Well! Let them accept, I cannot support an unholy course. I detest injustice and acrimonious acts.

Osama: Young man, you don"t seem to understand that, the repulsive smells of the skunk is etched inside her.

Okengwu: Oh! So the stench of rotten meat is engendered by embedded bacteria.

Osama: You are right, my in-law.

Okengwu: Um…Osama…um…I beg to leave now, the day has eaten deep. The birds are locating their nest. The hens have gone to roost. The bogey of the blackguard and the bode of the blizzard demand that I should leave right now.

Osama: ...um…Okengwu, you should have known that, I"m a philistine, so next time do not waste your time with rhetoric. Your wily allegory cum Ballard can"t make me legless to the extent of not reminding you of your role in the funeral of your mother-in-law in a few days to come.

Okengwu: [owlishly.] Well-spoken, Osama! Let"s see what the days ahead will look like. This is not the right time for bauble oration or high sounding nothing. It is not our desire to encounter Road hogs while driving on the road. I"m on my way home, goodbye.

Osama: [as Okengwu leaves, began to soliloquize.] Ehn, em! What does he mean by *what the days ahead will look like?* Whether he likes it or not, he must play his assigned role or else he will regret being our in-law. Ah! We are not ready to hear tales by moonlight from anyone o. Well! Let"s wait and see his new vista of intrigues. Um…um… yes! Somebody should warn him to desist from making noise about his taking care of my mother"s ailment o. Mm! I know what he wants to achieve, ugh! So, Okengwu tends to make us look irresponsible before the public. He can"t succeed. *isiewu* (goat head)!

Okengwu: [at home, pondering.] Chei! Chei!! I"m finished! What manner of in-laws do I have? The worst is yet to come from these greedy black guards. …um…upon all what I did for them, all I received in return was leer and ribald. May *Chiokike* save me from the fangs and claws of these black widows and hawks?

Scene 8

Epilogue

Two months later

Obidike: [at the Ogboto-Ukwu, addressing the people of Rumuoma.] Em, my people, as I was saying, we have heard the confession of Nmabaraego before she gave up the ghost after suffering from paranoids and eventually died of Parkinson"s disease. We have also heard of Nwadinobi, who is on his sick bed suffering from the same sickness. Death has refused to terminate his agony for now. We have witnessed the untimely demise of his loved ones recently. What a tragedy? What a pain, you may say?

The people: Nnanyi, we are not in sympathy with them o. This serves them right. The evil that men and women do lives with them nowadays. The god of retribution is on a divine mission to sanitize our society. Why should a man do juju (charm) and go into a covenant with the devil, in order to live forever, at the expense and peril of his loved ones? You see, their plight will serve as a deterrent to would-be blackguards.

Obidike: My people, you are right, but we have to forgive them, if they repent and apologise for their deeds against our *mores*.

The People: [cut in.] Nnanyi! We are tired of this family. Don"t you see that their actions have polluted our community? The youngsters amongst them are even doing the worst things. Their diabotical activities have compelled other communities to see us in a bad light. Nwadinobi and his children have turned this community into loamy soil for the germination of bastards cum rascals. Why should we be terrorized in our own enclave?

Obidike: Em! My people! Please, to err is human, but to forgive is divine. Let *Chiokike* take charge of our battle. Meanwhile, let"s ask Osama and his siblings, who are here right now, to apologize on behalf of their parents, especially Nwadinobi, and other members of his household. Osama! You can now mount the rostrum.

Osama: [fretfully.] I must tell everyone present that you are all half-wit. What sort of apology are you talking about? What are we to apologize for? Is it wrong for one to respond to a hypnotic-bogey inside him? If I may ask, can one challenge his *chi* (personal god) to a bout? I believe the future will teach you all a great lesson, for my parents chastised you with ordinary *koboko* (whips), I will chastise you with *akpi* (scorpions).

Obidike: [began to ponder like other elders present.] Chei! We are finished in this community o. What will be the fate of our children with these children of *Ekwensu*, hovering around? Hmm! So, we are yet to experience the worst scene of macabre?

The People: Nnanyi! We hope you have heard him? Are you still going to plead on the behalf of this unholy family?

Obidike: My people, I have heard him o. Em, you see! The snake can only beget a long thing. Can the zebra discard its strip? What a rat? Chei! We were moaning over the activities of the hawk but today the vampire is here before us. What a bogey trait? Mm! a recalcitrant fly follows the corpse to the grave…um…um…

Osama: [cut in before he left the scene.] Hey! If you like, reel out all the idiomatic expressions in this world, that‟s your own cup of tea. I have said what I wanted to say and our stand remains unchanged. I have to rat on (desert) this unholy gathering.

The People: [rambling in disgust.] Nnanyi, it‟s high time we apprise Nwadinobi and his ménage that no person or family is greater than the community. Yes! He, who refused to realize that Umunna is an acute waist pain that ought to be treated with care, will live to swallow the bitter pills.

Obidike: My people, now that the stubborn fly has perched on the scrotum and refuses to rat on, what do we do?

The People: Ah! Nnanyi! The fly is not on the scrotum o! Or are you still in sympathy with that unholy family after their impish deeds and Osama‟s scathing remarks on all of us?

Obidike: Em, my people, I beckon to you not to misconstrue my remarks. It is the human spirit in me that is insisting on forgiveness despite their unrepentant stand. Well! My personal feelings cannot be construed as that of the people.

The People: Nnanyi, we appreciate your feelings, but we have had enough from Nwadinobi‟s ménage.

Obidike: …um…now, what measure are we going to take to checkmate these unholy trends in our midst? Yes, ours is an egalitarian society, where *Óhàkárási* (what the people say) reigns supreme.

The People: Nnanyi, we should ostracize Nwadinobi and his household. Yes, O! They should be ex-communicated as outlaws and outcasts (friendless persons). None of us will interact with them in any way whatsoever. They ought to be declared *personae non grata* in any of our communal and personal activities. They are to carry the fetters and cross of the dejected homeless Homo sapiens.

Obidike: Are you saying with one voice that we should impose *Íkpikiri-ñkwú* (all round sanction) on them?

The People: Yááh!!! That is our stand. No shaking!

Obidike: Em, based on *Óhàkárási*, henceforth, the family of Nwadinobi is ostracized. They should be treated like outcasts, which they have inherited as a result of their diabolical activities. More importantly, nobody should attend or participate in the funeral rites of any of them, let them bury themselves. I hope this is what *Óhàkárá* (what the people said)?

The People: Yéáh!!! Nnanyi, your analysis is in order. That is our stand, enough of these impish activities in our society.

Nnanyereugo: [one of the elders, cut in.] Hey! My people, you see! He who refuses to recognize or acknowledge that *Igwebuike* (majority is strength) will live to see the fangs of solitariness. Em, can a man with one hand, have a good bath?

The People: Never!!! Nnanyi, this is a great word of wisdom.

Nnanyereugo: Yes! *Chiokike* knows why he gave us two eyes, two hands, two ears and two legs, amongst others, for none can function efficiently as a lone ranger. Can one person cook for a whole community and expect oddment?

The People: Never!!! Nnanyi.

Nnanyereugo: Verily, I tell you, no one individual can consume a meal (nosh) prepared by the entire community and live to say, "I"m grateful, this is a sumptuous and moorish meal".

The People: Chei! Nwadinobi! The anathema of a community. Ewuoh! *Ajo nwa* (imp).

Obidike: Ehn! My people, it is enough, *Chiokike* had already noted your frustration and agony in the hands of Nwadinobi, the enigmatic-anathema of our community and the stubborn TseTse fly that perched on the scrotum and refuses to rat on. If you attempt to hit it, you would probably hit your scrotum which is painful. But if you allow it to stay, it sucks your blood and makes you fall sick and uncomfortable.

The people: Mm!!! We have heard you, Nnanyi. We believe that *Chiokike* will frustrate this black leg and his ménage in our midst.

Obidike: Em! My people, the birds are locating their nest and the hen is roosting. In the absence of any other business, may we call it a day? Goodbye.

Scene 9

Three Weeks Later

The news of Nwadinobi"s demise broke and bruited abroad but his Umunna did not attend the funeral as agreed in their previous gathering in compliance with the *Íkpikiri-ñkwú* otherwise called Ostracization.

GLOSARY

Iwa-akwa - Tying Cloth ceremony which reflects initiation into manhood in Igbo cosmology.

Igbu-ichi - Cutting of the forehead as initiation into spiritual leadership cult. Ígbú íchí is a painful scarification in which the participant(s) went into sepsis or hemorrhage and 'died' to survive the fourteen days healing process after which he will re-emerge as both man to himself and a spirit man. Men who undergo scarification and proceed through all the rituals of title taking of the highest level (ichizu mmuo) are known as Ndichie (ancestors).

Nnanyi - My lord. It is also a reference to an elderly person.

Ofe egusi - Egusi Soup

Ugu - Vegetable (fruited pumpkin)

Nri ji - Yam food or pounded yam

Chiokike - God of creation

Chei! - Exclamation mark

Chi - Guardian angel or personal god.

Eze ji - King of yam or a great yam farmer with great barn full of yam tubers.

iséé - Amen

Mazi - Mister (Mr.)

Ńnọọ - well done

Ya gazie - Let it be well

Yááá	-	Yes or cheers of approval
Ndichie	-	Ancestors
Ichie	-	The Aged
Nsiko	-	Crab
Ugba	-	Oil bean
Nkwu-elu	-	Wine tapped from a standing palm tree
Ukazi	-	A special leaf use in the preparation of soup
Okporoko	-	Stock fish
Nwannedinamba	-	Good neighbourliness
Chiomumu	-	God of procreation
Chi ihu n' anya	-	God of love
Chi idi n'otu	-	God of unity or oneness
Chieweta edozie	-	God of protection
Ìbo – uzò	-	Clearing of road
Dinta	-	Hunter
Chineke	-	God of creation

Idinma	-	You are good
Diochie	-	Palm wine taper
Dokinta	-	Doctor
Umundomi	-	Women folk
Nte	-	Cricket
Umunna	-	Kinsmen
Nkelu	-	An illus at bird
Aruéméé	-	A sacrilege has been committed
Erima	-	A network of blood relations
Óhàkárási	-	Democracy
Íkpikiri-ñkwú	-	All round sanction or ostracization

About The Author

Korieocha Emmanuel Uwa is a native of Umunnam-Umuokeh in Obowo L.G.A. of Imo State. He attended Central School Amainyi-Ukwu and Uboma Secondary School, Ikperejere-Etiti, all in the present-day Ihitte-Uboma L.G.A. of Imo State. He had his higher educational training at the University of Uyo, Akwa Ibom State. He is an independent researcher and public affairs analyst, combating corrupt practices and autarchy, via his writings and articulated articles in the mass media besides his métier and list for adventures. He was also on the staff of Hallmark National Newspaper and National Mirror Newspaper, Lagos between 2005 and 2009 as Head of Sub-Editing Desk before joining The Accelerator Newspaper as the Copy/Online Editor between 2009 to 2011. He also worked as Production Editor at News Star Newspaper between 2011 to 2013. He later joined ASPA POP Investment Limited as the General Manager in 2013 to date.

Contact: nzekanzeone@gmail.com, tel: +2348059164101, +2348091968154

About The Book

Axiomatically, there is time for everything, so was the time for ***Dikeoha*** to get married. Bizarrely, as fate would superintend, ***Ekechi*** his betrothed got impregnated by a kleptomaniac.

As crackbrained as the scenario may seem, ***Dikeoha*** (being blinded by the aroma of love) forged ahead and married ***Ekechi***, who later gave birth to an imp, christened ***Nwadinobi***. This imp did not only devastated ***Dikeoha*** and his ménage but the entire people of Rumuoma and beyond.

This melodrama, albeit a fact of life, strives to depict the sordid realities associated with the act of marrying a woman with another man"s baby in her womb. A real dude ought to avoid such temptation; hence, *'the snake will at all time give birth to something of long thin limbless body with large mouth, forked tongue and fang'*. The story, more than any other, showcases how a singular goof in one"s life can destabilize a race. Do not make decisions that you will live to regret later.

Ingram Content Group UK Ltd.
Milton Keynes UK
UKHW020635060623
422954UK00014B/707